Halloween: The Curse Of Michael Myers

Howard Mahmood

FADE IN:
INT. DUNGEON - TUNNELS - NIGHT (DISTORTED)
The agonizing SCREAMS continue as we MOVE rapidly through a labyrinth of winding underground tunnels. Glowing torches light the way. Blurry, indistinct silhouettes of grim FIGURES wearing black cowled robes flash along the dank, craggy walls.

As we BLAST around dark corners, we realize we are looking from the P.O.V. of a SCREAMING young woman being pushed forward on a gurney. Plunging deeper into this hellish maze.

A door is SLAMMED. Wooden. Heavy. Muffling the SCREAMS.

Spurs CLANK on a pair of silver tipped cowboy boots as a
MYSTERIOUS STRANGER steps into VIEW. Long black duster.
Widebrimmed fedora. Lit cigarette dangling between gloved fingers.

INT. BIRTHING CHAMBER - NIGHT (CONTINUOUS)
A rat scampers from a hole, foraging in the muck of a rotted rack. A white sheet, saturated with blood, covers the parted legs of JAMIE LLOYD, now 16, cheeks flushed with perspiration.

JAMIE
Oh, God, it's coming! It's coming!

MARY, a young midwife, rushes in with a bowl of hot water. Jamie lurches, knocking the bowl out of the girl's hands; it SHATTERS on the floor.

JAMIE
(continuing)
Mary, mother of God, please make it stop!

Mary's face is frozen in horror. Jamie's SCREAMS build to an unnerving crescendo. The paiin too much for her to bear.

Lurid SHOCK CUTS from the previous "Halloween" entries a surrealistic blend of IMAGES and VOICES as Jamie relives her terrifying childhood ordeal:

LOOMIS (V.O.)
... Ten years ago he tried to kill Laurie
Strode ...

A) LAURIE STRODE (Jamie Lee Curtis) twists and squirms as she is strangled mercilessly in the hands of the murderous SHAPE.

LOOMIS (V.O.)
... Now he wants her daughter.

B) Trapped in her bedroom, 10 YEAR OLD JAMIE (Danielle Harris) struggles to open the door. She flings it open. The Shape is standing there, knife poised to kill!

LOOMIS (V.O.)
Michael Myers is here to kill that little girl and anyone else who gets in his way!

C) RACHEL (Ellie Cornell) dies in anguish as the Shape plunges a pair of scissors through her chest. TINA (Wendy Kaplan) dives right into the path of the Shape's knife. "Jamie, run!!!"

D) Jamie sinks to her knees behind the fallen Shape, taking its hand in her own. CLOSE ON the Shape's hand. Fingers flexing to life. A grotesque BRAND on its wrist an inverted isocsceles triangle that will come to be known as the mark of THORN.

E) BLINDING EXPLOSION rips through cinderblock. A jail cell blown to oblivion. FIRESTORM rages. The MYSTERIOUS STRANGER appears, opening fire with a SEMI AUTOMATIC RIFLE.

Pitiful wails of death. OFFICERS writhing in pools of blood. In the aftermath of this carnage stands YOUNG JAMIE.

INT. CHAMBER - NIGHT (SAME)

Jamie struggles against her bonds. Pushing. SCREAMING. Lapsing in and out of consciousness during the excruciating pangs of labor. Haunted by low, moaning VOICES. CHANTING.

EXT. POLICE STATION - BACK ALLEY - NIGHT (NEW FOOTAGE)

RESUME Jamie, filled with repidation as she staggers through the smoke filled cell into a darkened, drizzly alleyway.

JAMIE'S P.O.V.

Beyond the clearing wisps of smoke, THREE FIGURES wearing black ski masks usher THE SHAPE arms and legs shackled in heavy chains into the back of a white van.

BACK TO SCENE

Mutely terrified, Jamie backs away into the arms of another figure, obscured by smokescreen: the Mysterious Stranger!

Jamie's scream is cut off as the Stranger descends upon her like the Angel of Death.

A cigarette arcs throug the darkness like a tiny flare. Crushed under the boot of the Stranger.

A moment later, Jamie is shoved into the front seat of the van.

Doors SLAM. Tires SCREECH over wet pavement.

THE ENTIRE PRECINCT EXPLODES IN A HUGE CONFLAGRATION!
SHOCK
INT. CHAMBER - NIGHT

A SLAP and the first cry of the newborn BABY. Jamie sobs uncontrollably, the straps preventing her from reaching him.

JAMIE
Please ... give him to me ...

The infant is wrapped in black swaddling. The wooden door CREAKS open. Jamie's eyes fill with horror as the shadow of the Stranger fills the room. Standing at the threshold. Waiting to receive the child.

JAMIE
(continuing)
No, please ... my baby!
The dark sentinels march out in somber procession, ignoring her desperate pleas. Torches lighting the way.

JAMIE
(continuing)
Damn you!! Damn you all to hell!!!
Jamie's heartrending SHRIEKS are cut off by the cold sound of the

SLAMMING DOOR.
FADE TO BLACK.
MAIN TITLE SEQUENCE
A diaphanous column rises, a ghostly, slow motion cylinder of flame that BURNS through the SCREEN to form the MAIN TITLE:

HALLOWEEN
The OPENING CREDITS are BRANDED against the BLACK SCREEN by an invisible, kenetic force, interspersed with a SERIES OF CUTS:
Jamie's baby is lain upon a primitive altar. Ringed by eleven stones engraved with cryptic markings.
Hooded, faceless figures. Torches held aloft. Disembodied
VOICES. Whispering. Invoking a dark spell.
MARY, the young midwife, peers around a corner. Eyes glazed with horror. Watching. Spying.
The newborn SCREAMS. The flattened blade of a dagger smears a triangular symbol in blood over the baby's torso.
We MOVE IN on this symbol, capturing it in FREEZE FRAME. It burns off into fiery cinders, disintegrating into DARKNESS.
Silence. Then a startling CLAP OF THUNDER as we

SHOCK
A SIGN POST standing askew in a matted patch of lawn. WIND and RAIN. INTENSE FLASH of LIGHTNING illuminates:
"For Sale By Strode Realty SOLD"

EXT/INT. MYERS HOUSE - SUBJECTIVE P.O.V.
MOVE along a trail of drowning toys baseball, Power Rangers, a deck of Pogs TOWARD a weather beaten porch. Leftover gallons of Sears Best. Brushes soaking in turpentine. A dozen or so 2 x
2s l;ined up to replace a row of broken railing slats.
P.O.V. LOOKS UP to the tall, brooding edifice. Address reads: 45
Lampkin Lane. Fresh coat of white paint over old clapboard. New shutters on the narrow windows. A jack o' lantern grins behind filmy curtains. The Myers house.
Despite its recent face lift, it looks just as foreboding as it did in "Halloween I."

P.O.V. stalks down the side of the house, around to the back door. Opens it and quietly MOVES inside.

P.O.V. MOVES across the darkened kitchen. A drawer is opened.

LIGHTNING reveals a large butcher knife being withdrawn.

P.O.V. glides past the living room a few boxes, furniture to be arranged and MOVES swiftly UP a long flight of stairs.

Down the long, dark hallway ... through a door. A bedroom.

P.O.V. FINDS 6 year old DANNY STRODE ... tossing and turning in the throes of a nightmare.

An ear splitting THUNDER CRASH causes the boy to bolt upright in bed, looking right into the P.O.V. Sweating. Shaking.

Petrified.

DANNY'S P.O.V.
The THUNDER seems to ROAR from the ferocious jaws of T REX a
24" scale model posing on a shelf among an army of Jurassic monsters. Seemingly brought to life by the ELECTRICAL STORM.

FOLLOW DANNY as he leaps out of bed and pads across polished wooden floors into the hallway. LIGHTNING FLASHES. With the next THUNDER CRASH comes a startling, barely intelligible VOICE.

WHISPERING VOICE (O.S.)
Danny ...
Danny freezes. Slowly turns.

DANNY'S POV
An ominous shadow at the end of the hall, illuminated by
LIGHTNING. Long duster and brimmed hat. The Stranger! In his outstretched hand, the gleaming butcher knife!

WHISPERING VOICE (O.S.)
Kill for him!

BACK TO SCENE
Danny screams! THUNDER CRASHES HELLISHLY. Lights flash on.
Doors fly open. Suddenly Danny is swept up in the protective arms of his mother, KARA, 22.

KARA
Danny!
The little boy holds onto her for dear life. Crying hysterically. Eyes clenched tightly.

KARA
(continuing)
Shh. Mommy's here. What is it?

DANNY

The voice man! He's here!

Kara looks in the direction he's pointing. In the light there's just an antique coat rack "dressed" in a hat, rain jacket and old silver tipped umbrella.

KARA

Danny, no one's there.

Danny dares to look but now only cries harder.

Kara carries Danny back to his room, averting the steely eyed gaze of her father, JOHN STRODE, staunch, late 40s, wearing boxer shorts and a well worn undershirt.

JOHN

Some of us have to get some sleep around here. What's with that kid?

Kara ignores him as her mother, DEBRA, careworn face with compassionate eyes, tries to lend a hand.

DEBRA

Let me take him for you, Kara.

KARA

It's all right, Mom. Go back to bed.

Debra sighs resignedly. TIM, 18, stocky and streetwise, wearing torn red sweat pants and "Ice T" t shirt, casually replaces his
Walkman headphones and returns to his room.

INT. DANNY'S BEDROOM - NIGHT (A FEW MINUTES LATER)

Kara opens the closet and switches on the light. Satisfying Danny that it's empty, she breaks into her perfunctory routine.

KARA

Stay away monters, stay away ghouls. Stay away from Danny. You jerks know the rules.
(crossing to Danny's bed)
Better?

Danny giggles as his pretty young mother tucks him in.

DANNY

Mommy, when can we go home?

Kara sighs. They've been through this one before.

KARA

Home is here in Grandma and Grandpa's new house. At least while I'm in college. Remember our deal.

DANNY

The kids at school said this is a haunted house that a bad man used to live here.

KARA
They did, did they? Since when did we start listening to the kids at school?

DANNY
But I've seen him!

KARA
You've been watching too much TV.

DANNY
He says things. Bad things.

KARA
Like what?
Danny is afraid to tell her.

KARA
(continuing)
If you mean the things Grandpa says sometimes, ignore him. Once he gets to know you he'll come around ... Let the bad things you hear slide right off your back.
Kara tousles his blond hair and kisses his forehead. Then she goes to the closet, just about to turn out the light

DANNY
(sitting up; panicked)
No, Mom keep it on!

KARA
Okay ... But just for tonight.
Kara adjusts the closet door, causing one of Danny's school drawings to fly off the wall. She picks it up on her way out.

KARA
(continuing)
Good night, Danny.
Kara softly closes the door. Danny lies awake, blankets drawn up to his chin, eyes wide. Still very much afraid.

INT. KARA'S ROOM (CONTINUOUS)
Kara yawns, removes her glasses and rubs her eyes, setting Danny's drawing on a pile of open books. Cliffs Notes and Diet Coke cans. Telltale signs of a late night cram session.
Adjusting the dial on her FM/alarm clock, Kara begins to move about the little room, slipping out of her clothes as the subtly seductive voice of a WOMAN comes over the radio:

WOMAN (V.O.)
I know this sounds crazy, Harry, but I love him. I write to him every week. I think I even want to have his child
The woman is cut off by the nasally, steel trap voice of HARRY
SIMMS, talk radio's most popular man of controversy:

HARRY SIMMS (V.O.)
Let me get this straight, Debi. Now you're saying that not only does this guy get you sexually aroused, but now you want to bear his offspring?!
Wearing only her bra and panties, Kara moves to a full length mirror and lets down her long, flaxen hair. Beneath her studious exterior, she is quite attractive: delicate features with an enviable, naturally toned figure.

WOMAN (V.O.)
Deep down, he's just like you and me. He just needs someone to understand him. Someone to love him.

HARRY SIMMS (V.O.)
You're talking about one of this nation's most notorious serial killers like he belongs in some kind of Est seminar! What planet have you been on, lady? Michael Myers has been dead for six years!
A CLICK as the woman is abruptly DISCONNECTED.
Kara suddenly whirls around, startled by a FLASH of something a face in the mirror! Drawn to the window behind her, she rubs off rainy mist and peers outside.

KARA'S P.O.V. of the large Victorian frame house directly across the street.
Another FLASH OF LIGHTNING reveals the shadow of a man standing in the uppermost window looking right at her!

ANGLE ON KARA
Frightened, her eyes lock on Danny's drawing. A child's scribbling in red Crayon: The triangular symbol of Thorn!

EXT. MYERS HOUSE / BLANKENSHIP HOUSE
Kara draws the priscilla curtains over the window as we PULL BACK through the pouring RAIN ... toward the house across the street.
An ornate sign on the front door reads:
"Blankenship House Rooms Available"
CRANE UP toward the window where the shadowy figure stands. An insidious CRASH OF THUNDER as we PUSH through the window.

INT. TOMMY'S APARTMENT - NIGHT (CONTINUOUS)
A macabre display of old newspaper headlines, arranged helterskelter on a wall: "HALLOWEEN KILLS ESCAPES FROM ASYLUM."

"HORROR IN HADDONFIELD: MICHAEL MYERS CLAIMS 16 LIVES."
"REIGN
OF TERROR ENDS AS MYERS PERISHES IN VIGILANTE EXPLOSION."
Harry Simms BOOMS over a state of the art HiFi system. A cassette tape RECORDS the continuing broadcast.

HARRY SIMMS (V.O.)
Now we've got someone who claims he's actually seen Michael Myers. Does this whacko caller have a name?
Staring out the window at the Myers house, TOMMY DOYLE, a strapping 25 year old with reddish brown hair and intense eyes, cradles a cordless phone.

TOMMY
My name's Tommy. I was only eight years old when I saw him. But I was lucky. I survived.
Tommy paces nervously around his sparsely furnished attic apartment. Classic horror movie one sheets and mint first edition comic books share wall space with a chilling array of guns, knives, and survivalist weapons.

HARRY SIMMS (V.O.)
Sounds like you're a candidate for electroshock therapy, Tommy. Don't tell me after all this time you still believe Myers is alive?!
Tommy pauses, mesmerized by one of the newspaper clippings.

TOMMY
Michael's work isn't finished in Haddonfield.
Now it's just a matter of time before he comes home to kill again. But this time I'll be ready.
MOVE IN TIGHT on the headline, frail and yellowed by age:
"November 1, 1978. TOMMY DOYLE SURVIVES BABYSITTER BLOODBATH."
Directly beneath this: "November 3, 1989. JAMIE LLOYD FEARED

DEAD IN POLICE STATION MASSACRE."
CLOSE ON a photograph of young Jamie and

SLOW DISSOLVE TO:
INT. DUNGEON - CHAMBER - NIGHT
Jamie remains strapped to the table, wrapped in bloody sheets.
Eyes closed. Deathly still. Suddenly an urgent, WHISPERING VOICE pierces the darkness:

WHISPERING VOICE (O.S.)
Jamie? Jamie?!
Jamie startles awake to see the midwife frantically releasing her straps.

MARY

Come with me if you want to save your baby.

Jamie can't believe her eyes. Mary opens a threadbare knapsack revealing the baby inside!

A soul shuddering RUMBLE echoes throughout the cavern. Jamie leaps up, eyes wide with fear, sensing the evil presence.

JAMIE
Oh, God ... He's coming!

MARY
We've got to move. Now!

Pulsing with adrenaline, Jamie harnesses the knapsack over her shoulders and follows Mary out into the tunnels.

TUNNEL GATE
Chains GRIND over rusted pulleys. A massive iron gate rises, revealing a pair of filthy work boots. Legs planted in bold stance as a tall, ominous shape begins to emerge.

ANOTHER TUNNEL
The terrified midwife leads Jamie with her baby on a breathless flight through the winding network of tunnels. Haunted by the
ECHOING SOUNDS of the rising gate.

STALKING P.O.V. - THROUGH TUNNELS
Gliding forward into the hollow catacombs. Slow by determined.
Sensing the way.

ANOTHER PART OF THE TUNNELS
Reaching a corner, Mary stops and sends Jamie off in the opposite direction.

MARY
There! It's that way!

JAMIE
No

MARY
Save your baby go now!

Jamie runs, disappearing down the dark tunnel. Mary quickly removes her shoes and tears off, now SILENT.

STALKING P.O.V. surges around a corner. FINDS Mary. MOVES IN on her.

ANOTHER ANGLE
Mary turns in small circles. Fear mounting as she falters into darkness. Heavy, labored BREATHING fills the tunnel.

A mask the pale, neutral features of a man weirdly distorted by the rubber materialized out of the void right behind her. THE

SHAPE!
Mary turns, about to scream when the Shape lunges out, lifts her up by the nape of the neck and SLAMS her forehead into a large metal SPIKE jutting out from the cavern wall!
Leaving her impaled like a fish on a hook, the Shape resumes its relentless pursuit. Eerie under the lighted torches.

END OF TUNNEL
Jamie runs frantically. Methodical, heavy FOOTSTEPS behind her.
She chances a look behind. The Shape is coming!
Jamie vaults up a dark stairwell. A trap door above. It won't budge. Jamie frantically POUNDS against the hatch.
The Shape mounts the stairs!
Strength fueled by sheer desperation, Jamie forces the door open.
Tumbles onto muddy ground.

EXT. WOODS - NIGHT
Jamie drags herself out of the hole and half runs, half stumbles with her baby through an ugly, charred forest. Sharp branches whip at her face. RAIN falls. LIGHTNING streaks across the sky.
As if hell spawned, the Shape emerges from the underground chamber and trudges forward, bold and unstoppable.
Jamie tumbles into a gully, nearly dropping the knapsack. She picks herself up, hands groping at rain sopped earth. The Shape is right behind her!

INT. PICKUP TRUCK - NIGHT (SAME)
A slap happy, overweight MOTORIST sips coffee from a 7 11 cup, straining to see the road through falling rain and fogged up glasses. Harry Simms keeps him mindlessly occupied.

HARRY SIMMS (V.O.)
Next up is Dwayne. What's on your feeble excuse for a mind, "Dwayne?"
The Motorisft lets out a hardy GUFFAW, spilling his coffee.

MOTORIST
Shit!
Fingers burning, he searches the glove compartment for a napkin.

DWAYNE (V.O.)
I'd just like to say that I listen to your show every night, Harry. I think you're the best. I can't tell you how excited we are that you'll be paying a visit to our little town tomorrow night.

HARRY SIMMS (V.O.)
Do you have a point to make here, Dwayne, or should I just keep practicing my wrist exercises?

DWAYNE
(chortles)
Harry, you're too much. I'd just like to say that I understand how things have changed in the 90's. Gays in the military, cut off your husband's do jigger, become a national hero.
But I just can't see any sense in bringing
Halloween back to Haddonfield.
The Motorist looks up. Eyes go wide with panic. Startled GASP.

P.O.V. THROUGH WINDSHIELD
Jamie stands in the middle of the road, SCREAMING bloody murder.

EXT. WOODED ROAD / INT. PICKUP TRUCK (SAME)
Tires SCREECH. The pickup stops on a dime. The Motorist just sits there, mouth agape as the shrieking girl throws open the door and clambers into the passenger seat.

JAMIE
Drive! Goddamnit, drive!
Through his side view mirror, the unsuspecting Motorist sees the outline of a quickly approaching man. Unrolling his window, he rubbernecks a look outside.

MOTORIST
Hey, what do you think you're
CRUNCHING BONE and TEARING FLESH as the Shape's hands shoot through the window, twisting the man's head off his shoulders!
Jamie SCREAMS! Lunges for the steering wheel. Slams her foot down hard on the gas.

ANOTHER ANGLE
The pickup bullets forward, fishtailing up the road, never slowing down as the driver's door flies open, dumping the motorists's headless bulk into a muddy ditch.

INT. PICKUP (SAME)
Jamie drives. Checks to see that her baby is safe. Then lets out a PRIMAL SCREAM. A hysterical release of fear and rage, drowned out by the squabble of VOICES over the radio:

MALE CALLER #2 (V.O.)
You're coming here for this Halloween fair it's all just a game a publicity stunt for you, isn't it Harry? These kids they're not old enough to remember what Myers did here. They look up to you. Now you're just asking for trouble.

HARRY SIMMS (V.O.)

You people really get me. What are they putting in the water in that town?

INT. LOOMIS'S CABIN - NIGHT (SAME)
LIGHTNING FLASHES and RAIN pelts the windows of a bucolic cabin.
This is a man's retreat and has been for years. Dark wood, worn leather, a few tastefully chosen antiques. Floor to floor ceiling shelves containing a myriad of books and an impressive display of awards and degrees, all bearing the name: SAMUEL J. LOOMIS, Ph.D.
After a STATION IDENTIFICATION, "The Harry Simms Show" resumes, tinny voiced CALLERS blaring over a handsomely restored 1928
Bremer Tully.

MALE CALLER #3 (V.O.)
All these fanatics aside, Harry, I'd personally like to thank whoever did the masked one in. Saved us tax payers a lot of money in the long run.

FEMALE CALLER #3 (V.O.)
Yeah, that sucker's been dead for six years.
It's about time they had a Halloween revival in this town. Now my kids can stop driving me crazy!
MOVE IN behind a bald, sharp featured man, hunched over a can as he reminisces over a collection of framed photographs memories of his wife and children.

MALE CALLER #4 (V.O.)
What happened to that psychiatrist of his?
Loomis, I think was his name. I heard the old quack was dead.
Turning at the mention of his name is DR. LOOMIS himself, wearing spectacles, a comfortable sweater and his trademark goatee. For the first time ever, we actually see him smile. The burn scars on his face have all but faded away. Last traces of the horrid past.

LOOMIS
Not dead. Just very much retired.
Loomis hobbles to the desk and finishes cutting out a newspaper article. As he arranges the strips of paper in a leather bound scrapbook, a sudden KNOCK at the door gives him a startle.

EXT. LOOMIS'S CABIN - NIGHT (SAME)
An ominous FIGURE, clad in hat and trench coat, stands beneath the glowing porch light, silhouetted in the pouring RAIN.
Loomis opens the door, eyes straining in the semi darkness, trying to identify his unexpected visitor.

LOOMIS
(sudden recognition)
What the devil?! Come in come in!

INT. LOOMIS'S CABIN - NIGHT (CONTINUOUS)

Shuffling inside, dripping with rain, DR. TERENCE WYNN, a well dressed gentleman in his 50s, removes his hat and coat, quickly making himself at home by the crackling fire.

WYNN
Christ, what a night! Not even so much as a sign for five miles on that road!

LOOMIS
That's the whole idea of living in the country. I thrive on the seclusion.

Wynn heads for the kitchen, rummaging through cabinets and drawers as Loomis dutifully wipes up his muddy trail.

WYNN (O.S.)
Don't tell me that the reviled Rasputin of
Smith's Grove has grown complacent in his golden years. I don't buy it for a single second, Dr. Loomis.

Loomis immediately senses that Wynn has an angle.

LOOMIS
And in all these years, I've never known you to make house calls, Dr. Wynn. Especially at this hour ...

Wynn returns with a bottle of Irish whiskey and two shot glasses.
Thrusts one in Loomis's hand and begins to pour.

WYNN
Unlike you, Sam, I learned many years ago not to second guess the motives of my fellow man.
Remember what Freud said: 'Sometimes a cigar is just a cigar.' Or, in this case, a drink is just a drink.

LOOMIS
I hope you didn't come all the way out here in this storm just to quote Freud.

WYNN
As always, your keen powers of perception astound me. And you're right. I've come to celebrate.
(raising his glass)
After thirty two years as Psychiatric
Administrator, guess who has been named
Smith's Groves new Chief of Staff.

LOOMIS
But surely Rogers isn't

WYNN
Retiring.
Loomis is abruptly stunned and delighted by the news.

LOOMIS
Why congratulations! I can think of no one better suited for the position.
The two old sparring partners drink to the occasion. But Wynn's angle soon comes to the helm.

WYNN
Of course, I need a new Administrator. Someone who can bring new life and some old blood, if you'll pardon the expression back to our program ...
Loomis prepares himself for the bomb.

WYNN
(continuing)
We need you, Dr. Loomis.

LOOMIS
You should know that it's not wise to play Halloween pranks on me.

WYNN
You're the only man for the job, Sam. Things haven't been the same since you left. I'm recruiting the best psychiatric team in the country. Old colleagues. This is your change to finally make a difference.
Loomis scratches his head and settles down into his comfortable easy chair, amused at the irony of Wynn's speech.

LOOMIS
Even after my stroke six years ago they practically had to hold a gun to my head to get me to retire. Now things have changed.
I've changed. The ghosts have been buried.
Why on earth would I want to dig them up again?
Loomis finally looks over at Wynn, surprised to find him standing at the desk, looking through his scrap book.

WYNN
Seems to me there's at least one ghost that's still lurking in your closet.
We follow Wynn's gaze down toward the open page. A blazing tabloid headline: "MICHAEL MYERS DEAD OR ALIVE?"

SHOCK
EXT. RURAL HIGHWAY - NIGHT
Jamie's getaway truck ROARS around a bend, tearing up a deserted stretch of highway. The STORM rages.

INT. PICKUP (CONTINUOUS)

Jamie strains to see as she drives through sheets of RAIN. Bone weary, fighting panic, holding one hand steady against the wheel, the other on the CRYING infant.

JAMIE
God ... Help us, please ...
Something up ahead. Jamie's face fills with expectancy.

JAMIE'S P.O.V. - THROUGH WINDSHIELD

A lighted sign appears out of the darkness. Glowing salvation.
Familiar red white and blue logo. "GREYHOUND."

EXT. BUS DEPOT - NIGHT

The pickup drives into the glow of orange vapor lights. SKIDS to a stop in a deserted parking lot. Jamie staggers out, cradling the knapsack as she runs toward the old depot.

INT. BUS DEPOT - NIGHT

Jamie blasts through double glass doors. But the bus station is devoid of life. Empty benches. Blank ARRIVAL/DEPARTURE signboard. The low hum of vending machines.
Jamie moves toward the ticket counter. A handwritten sign left by the attendant: "BACK IN 20."
Shivering, holding her baby, Jamie enters an old fashioned phone booth. Picks up the receiver and immediately dials 911.

VOICE (V.O.)
You have reached Haddonfield Emergency
Services. Due to severe weather conditions, all circuits are momentarily busy. If this is not an emergency, please dial directly ...
Jamie slams the phone down in terrified frustration. Suddenly she becomes aware of the radio program. Piped in over ancient loudspeakers:

HARRY SIMMS (V.O.)
For anyone who gives a flying circus, this is
Harry Simms the light in your night, the love of your loins and I want to hear from more of you bogeyman believers out there. So give me your best shot at 1 800 878 7274. That's 1 800 URTRASH!
The STATION IDENTIFICATION cuts in. Jamie picks up the receiver and frantically dials the number.

INT. LOOMIS'S CABIN - NIGHT (SAME)

Wynn doesn't give up the sales pitch even as Loomis leads him to the door. The radio program still squawking in the b.g.

WYNN

But with Rogers and his house of hacks gone, you'd make the rules. Just think it over.

LOOMIS
Please try to understand, Terence. I've already made up my mind.
As Wynn continues to talk, his voice trailing off into nothingness, Loomis's attention is diverted to the VOICES on the radio.

HARRY SIMMS (V.O.)
So they're trying to kill you and your baby.
Don't tell me. Your name also happens to be
Rosemary.

JAMIE (V.O.)
(intense whisper)
No please listen! They're coming ... coming for me and my baby.
Loomis's eyes widen; a man possessed.

HARRY SIMMS (V.O.)
Come on, sweetheart what is this? Who's coming?

JAMIE (V.O.)
It's ... Michael ...
(releasing)
... Michael Myers!
Loomis staggers. A lifetime of nightmares coming back to haunt him all at once.

INT. TOMMY'S APARTMENT - NIGHT (SAME)
PRESS IN TIGHT ON TOMMY in bed. Listening through headphones.
Sitting upright. Thunderstruck.

JAMIE (V.O.)
Somebody help me! Dr. Loomis, are you out there? Can you hear me?

INT. LOOMIS'S CABIN - NIGHT (SAME)
Wynn watches with rapt attention as Loomis unlocks his safe and withdraws a metal case. He pops it open, revealing his trusted .357
Magnum and a box of cartridges.

INT. BUS DEPOT - NIGHT (SAME)
A bus has arrived. The ATTENDANT returns to his post. Jamie hangs up the phone, filled with trepidation as PASSENGERS file inside. A strung out ROCKER. A pair of stern faced NUNS. A PRETTY TEENAGER greeted in the loving arms of her BOYFRIEND.
Just as she is about to step out of the phone booth, a TALL MAN, back turned, wearing a hat and black trench coat, moves to stand outside the booth! Jamie freezes.
Securing her baby in the knapsack, Jamie throws open the door.

Suddenly the Tall Man steps in her path!

TALL MAN
Are you all right, young lady?
Shaking uncontrollably, Jamie shrinks away. Backing down a narrow hall through the door marked "LADIES ROOM."

INT. LADIES ROOM - NIGHT (SAME)
Water runs into a grimy basin. Unable to contain her tears, she washes the newborn. Takes a roll of paper towels and tries to rub the triangular blood mark off his chest. Suddenly the lights go out. Jamie gasps. Clutching her baby, she turns off the faucet and melts into the darkness.
The door CREAKS open. FOOTSTEPS echo inside.

JAMIE has locked herself inside one of the stalls. Heart pounding. The FOOTSTEPS grow louder. Jamie's eyes dart frantically.

STALKING P.O.V.
MOVING methodically past the row of stalls, pushing open each door, revealing that they are all empty. A CRASH from the last stall.
P.O.V. moves toward it. RUSTLING and MOVEMENT inside.
A HAND pushes on the door. An open window above the toilet. Jamie is gone!

EXT. BUS DEPOT - NIGHT (CONTINUOUS)
Jamie trembles off a stack of crates piled beneath the window and dashes around the side of the depot.
Suddenly the bus ROARS by, sending up a muddy wave as it pulls out, disappearing down the highway.
Jamie moves swiftly across the parking lot, clutching the knapsack.
She throws open the door of the pickup and jumps into the driver's seat.

INT. PICKUP - NIGHT (CONTINUOUS)
Slapping down the locks, Jamie thrusts the key into the ignition.
The engine REVS to life. She guns it, peeling out of the parking lot. Back toward the highway.
She drives on, suppressing her tears, stealing glances at the knapsack bunched up on the passenger's seat. Then she turns and looks forward with concentrated attention.

JAMIE'S P.O.V.
A sign looms ahead: "Haddonfield Memorial Hospital 10 Mi."

BACK TO SCENE
Jamie sighs with relief, steadying the wheel just as
HIGHBEAMS flash on right behind her, a juggernaut roaring out of blackness! Jamie's eyes flood with terror.

JAMIE'S P.O.V. - THROUGH WINDSHIELD
The grill of a familiar white van shoots forward, SLAMMING violently against the pickup's rear bumper.

JAMIE is jolted forward in her seat. Holding on the wheel with a white knuckle grip as she's repeatedly hit from behind.

EXT. HIGHWAY - NIGHT
The unseen madman noses forward, veering sharply over the double yellow line, scraping sides with the truck.
Headlights sear a path through the night, locked in neck and neck profile. SPARKS flashing at 70 miles per hour.
The van forces Jamie onto the shoulder. It leaves the road, tearing branches from trees. Jamie SCREAMING.

EXT. PUMPKIN PATCH - THE CHASE
A quick cut MONTAGE, events ticking out in fractions of a second like a nightmare:
The pickup springboards over a gulch and slams down hard, tires spinning in waves of mud, careening through a vast field. A pumpking patch.
The van reappears in a glare of headlights. Its engine screaming with fire breathing rage. The pickup puts on a furious burst of speed. Eating up pumpkins and spinning out chunks of splattering seeds and pulp.
The van bears down hard, slingshotting across the field, whizzing past the pickup, cutting right in front of it.

INT. PICKUP
Something heavy is thrown from the back of the van right through the windshield!
Glass EXPLODES! Jamie SCREAMS, hands going up instinctively to protect her face. Swerving wildly out of control.
She looks to see a sprawling, mutilated corpse on top of her. Wide, cold, lifeless eyes Mary!

JAMIE
No!!!

EXT. PUMPKIN PATCH (CONTINUOUS)
The pickup rockets at breakneck speed toward the edge of the field.
Suddenly

JAMIE'S P.O.V.
The Shape stands in the field, tall and unmoving, white mask glowing hideously in the rush of oncoming headlights.

BACK TO SCENE
The truck plows into the Shape, dragging it under, SLAMMING headlong into the trunk of a huge oak tree.

Everything is abruptly and shockingly silent. Like a phantom in the night, the van is gone. The Shape nowhere to be seen.

Steam billows from the pickup, engine TICKING, a heap of shattered glass and mangled steel. Pinned against the base of the tree is a shape in human form a scarecrow!

MOVE IN on Jamie, face down against the steering wheel. Coughing on the noxious fumes, she stirs back to life. Slowly, painfully, she shoulders the door. Falls onto the ground.

A SPARK ignites. BLINDING FLASH as the gas tank EXPLODES, setting the truck ablaze. Jamie turns, her face a frozen rictus of horror.

Debris rains down on her.

Suddenly a grim shadow rises from the field. The Shape wielding an enormous butcher knife!

Jamie rolls onto her back, SCREAMING.

JAMIE
No NO!!!
Suddenly the knife plunges down and lands with a terrible THUD.

INT. PICKUP
The knapsack catches fire ... but inside there is no baby. Only a roll of paper towels from the bus depot.

THE SCARECROW burns; mocking Jamie with its grinning, hand painted face.

SLOW DISSOLVE TO:
THE SHAPE looks at us, white mask scintillating against blinding rays of SUNLIGHT. Rivulets of blood drip off a large carving knife.

PULLING BACK, we see it is a life sized, knife wielding effigy of Michael Myers, sitting astride the "For Sale by Strode Realty" sign. Stage blood spells out the words: "He's coming!"

EXT. MYERS HOUSE - MORNING (CONTINUOUS)
John Strode looks up with disgust as he inspects the grim monument that's been left on his front lawn during the night. Puffing on a cigarette, wearing slippers and a flimsy bath robe, John raises a large axe.

A group of neighborhood KIDS some dressed in Halloween costumes stand a safe distance away. Gathered on the sidewalk.

Gawking, whispering, tittering.

John angrily swings the axe into the signpost. The kids jump with a collective start.

JOHN
Enough ...
(one CHOP)
... of this ...
(two CHOPS)
... Michael Myers ...

(timber)

... shit!

Suddenly the sign crashes down and "Michael Myers" with it. The kids huddle. John turns on them, brandishing the axe.

JOHN
(continuing)
You stinkin' kids got three seconds to get the hell off my property! One, two

That's all it takes. The kids scatter, tripping over one another as they tear off down the black.

Satisfied with himself, John stubs out his cigarette and hauls the sign and its now headless rider to the trash.

Then he trudges up the porch steps, dropping the axe as he enters the house. Uttering oaths under his breath.

BOOM UP over the surrounding neighborheed. SUPERIMPOSE:

"Haddonfield, Illinois. Halloween."

Last night's storm has given way to an incredibly bright and picturesque morning. CHILDREN pour out of their homes, bursting with excitement, dressed in colorful costumes.

Even the Myers house, with its trimmed hedges and fresh coat of paint, somehow manages to look invite.

A white van slowly rolls up the street. WKNB logo, streamers and a large orange banner proclaiming: "HADDONFIELD JUNIOR COLLEGE

HARVEST FAIRE '95 See Harry Simms Live October 31." A now familiar voice booms over loudspeaker:

HARRY SIMMS (V.O.)
This is Hard Harry Simms harping on ya from the
Big Apple. Tonight's the night and the place to be is the First Annual Harvest Faire. So come on out of your broom closets, 'Fielders, and bogey the night away with me.

MALE CALLER #4 (V.O.)
Harry, I just won first prize for ugliest costume! Guess who I'm dressed as.

HARRY SIMMS (V.O.)
Your mother?

MALE CALLER #4 (V.O.)
No, man You!!!

EXT. SANITARIUM - MORNING
A car bearing an official state emblem stops outside an imposing curtain of security gates. A large sign reads: "SMITH'S GROVE

WARREN COUNTY SANITARIUM."

A hand reaches out and waves a plastic key card in front of an infrared scanner. Surveillance cameras perched on the walls.
As the gate yawns open and the car drives through, we SEE the asylum in the distance the entire perimeter bounded by woods and barbed wire fences.

INT. WYNN'S CAR (CONTINUOUS)
Wynn drives. Loomis in the passenger seat, fueling his own anxieties.

LOOMIS
It was her voice. On the radio. It was
Jamie. Calling for me.

WYNN
You don't know that for sure. It could have been anyone. A practical joke. Kids.

LOOMIS
It was Jamie Lloyd. She came back, as I knew she would one day. And whatever has brought her back has brought Michael back as well.

WYNN
After six years? Sam, she died with him in that explosion after the

LOOMIS
That's what someone wants us to believe, but I tell you Michael is alive. I feel him. I sense the evil that lives inside, just as I did all those years as I watched him. Sitting behind these very same walls. Staring. Growing stronger.
(off Wynn's silence)
As my colleague, as my friend, please. I can't go through this again. Not alone. I need your help to stop him.
Wynn stares. Loomis's words fall on him like a death sentence.

INT. SANITARIUM - RECEPTION AREA (SAME)
Gold insignia on mahogany doors: "TERENCE WYNN CHIEF OF STAFF."
Wynn and Loomis stride through a plush reception area. DAWN, an attractive, high energy secretary, keeps pace, taking notes, handing
Wynn his briefcase, phone messages, etc.

WYNN
Cancel all my appointments. Get Dr. Loomis anything he needs files, tests, records of every treatment ever administered to a former patient of ours Michael Myers.

DAWN
(stunned)
Michael Myers?
Wynn stops abruptly before heading out the door.

WYNN
That's right. We think there's a very good chance he might still be alive.
Loomis acknowledges Wynn's silent understanding.

CORRIDOR
Wynn and Loomis move along a sterile white corridor. Wynn uses his key card to BUZZ them through a series of metal security cages. A retinue of DOCTORS and NURSES fall in behind.

WYNN
(continuing)
Notify Haddonfield's sheriff; tell him we're on our way. I want the entire staff on alert. We go to code red lockdown for twenty four hours.
(beat)
If he is alive, I plan on bringing him back.

LOOMIS
Or what's left of him.
They cut down a sub passageway and out a fire exit.

EXT. SANITARIUM - LANDING FIELD (CONTINUOUS)
Loomis and Wynn dash across a windswept field where a Smith's Grove medical transport helicopter awaits them. The deafening WHINE of spinning rotors as a TECHNICIAN refuels.
The doctors step inside. The doors close and the helicopter lifts off, rising high above the cluster of the white coats below.

INT. MYERS HOUSE - KITCHEN - MORNING
A blender whips up a revolting concoction of chocolate Yoo Hoo, banana yogurt and chewy Gummi worms as Tim, wearing Levi's baggies and a "Harry Simms Kicks Ass" T shirt, raps on the phone.

TIM
Bro', I knew Harry when we lived in the city.
Don't worry he'll be there. We've got everything arranged. Get with me tonight at the fair and I'll hook you up. Peace.
Tim hangs up, guzzling down his shake as Debra navigates around him, setting out the breakfast dishes as Kara tries to study.
John, dressed in what might be a respectable business suit if it fit him better, mutters grumpily as he pours himself a cup of coffee.

JOHN
Shitheads ... Defacing my property. I showed them ...

DEBRA
Relax, John. They were just kids.

JOHN
Kids are what's ruining this country.
Everywhere you go, it's the same. No goddamn respect.
Tim lets out a huge BELCH as he finishes drinking his breakfast.

JOHN
(continuing)
See what I'm talkin' about?

DEBRA
You'll never pass that exam on an empty stomach, Kara.
Debra snatches the book out of Kara's hands.

DEBRA
(continuing; reading)
Cognitive Therapy and Emotional Disorders?
What are they teaching in college these days?
The art of going crazy?

KARA
(indignant)
It's called psychology, Mom. Living in this house is what's driving me crazy.

JOHN
Who the hell told you to come live here in the first place?
Kara rises, collects her books, trying to avoid a confrontation.

KARA
I'd better get Danny to school.

JOHN
She don't show her face for five years, then expects us to roll out the red carpet. You think going to college is gonna make up for your mistakes, girl?

DEBRA
John, please don't

TIM
Yo', just lay off her, Dad.
Suddenly Danny runs in, showing off in his dinosaur costume.
ROARING loudly. Startling John.

JOHN
What the fuck
Kara immediately seizes Danny's hand and ushers him toward the back door.

KARA
Let's go, Danny.

DEBRA
Kara, wait. John. Can't we all just sit down? Try to be a family for once?

KARA
I'm sorry, Mom.
Debra reaches into her purse and hands Kara a couple of dollars.

JOHN
That's it, Debra, keep slipping her the cash.
While you're at it, why don't you just give her all our goddamn money?!
John explodes, dumping the entire contents of her purse onto the floor. Debra recoils. Kara steps in. Danny is terrified.

KARA
Stay away from her, you bastard.

JOHN
(re Danny)
I only see one bastard in this house.
Kara flies at him with Medea like rage. John instantly grabs her by the neck and shoves her violently against the counter.

TIM
Dad! Let her go!

DEBRA
John! Stop it! Stop it!
Danny looks outside. Frozen in horror. A VOICE whispers.

WHISPERING VOICE (V.O.)
Kill him, Danny ... Kill him ...
Danny moves across the kitchen. Mesmerized. Through the screen door, the Shape can be seen standing in the back yard.
Kara's eyes bulge as John squeezes her throat. Choking her.

JOHN
You ever raise your hand to me again, I'll kill you, you understand?
John looks down to see the tip of a butcher knife pointed at his groin. Danny is holding it his eyes dark, emotionless. Ever so slowly, John releases Kara. Debra and Tim watch in horrified astonishment.
Suddenly there's a KNOCK at the back door. Kara dives toward

Danny. The knife clatters to the floor as she picks him up, grabs her book bag and hurtles outside.

EXT. MYERS HOUSE - BACK YARD (CONTINUOUS)
BETH, 19, very "retro," cute in the waifish sense milky white skin, two tone hair and a dangling nose ring is nearly bowled off the back porch as Kara and Danny fly out the door.

BETH
Make way for the Hardin County Express.
(following them across the yard)
Hey, where's Tim? We're supposed to go over the list of events for tonight
Beth is taken aback when she sees the bruise on Kara's neck.

BETH
(continuing)
He do that to you?

KARA
Another episode of 'Daddy Knows Best' at the Strode house.

BETH
Pig. What the hell happened this time?
Suddenly Tim jumps out from behind a clothesline, locking his arms around Beth, attacking her with kisses.

BETH
(continuing)
Hold on, hot lips. We got work to do.

TIM
Shit, Beth, why do we have to be the ones to organnize this friggin' fair? It's only Halloween.
Beth shoves the clipboard at him, a champion of her cause.

BETH
How many times o I have to tell you? It's not about Halloween. It's about being political. There are too many people with corn cobs up their ass in this town telling us what we can and can't do. If we want change, it's up to us to set an example.

INT. MYERS HOUSE - KITCHEN (SAME)
Debra is on the floor, stifling her tears, putting things back in her purse. John stares coldly out the window.

JOHN

I want her and that kid out of here tonight.
Debra rises, facing him scornfully.

DEBRA
I thought inheriting your father's house ... the business ... moving out here might change things. But you're still the same, John.
(with finality)
Kara has come home, and I'll be damned if I let you turn her away again.
Debra storms off. John bores holes into her with his eyes.

EXT. BLANKENSHIP HOUSE (SAME)
Tim lifts Danny into the back seat of Beth's convertible VW Bug plastered with "Greenpeace" and "This is Your Brain on Drugs" bumper stickers. Kara and Beth in front.

TIM
Whatever happened to women in back?

BETH
Reality check, dillweed. This is 1995.
Pulling away from the curb, Beth honks at MRS. BLANKENSHIP, at least 80, owner of the student boarding house across the street.

BETH
(continuing)
See you tonight, Mrs. Blankenship!
The old woman just stares forward. A gardem hose in hand as she waters a garden of long dead flowers.
Kara shields her eyes, distracted, looking up at the old Victorian house.

KARA'S P.O.V.
Beth drives down a shady, tree lined avenue, unaware of the white van that is following them.

KARA
Beth, who's that guy that lives across the hall from you?

BETH
Why? You interested?

KARA
No! I keep seeing him staring out his window.
Watching me.

BETH

You mean Tommy. Yeah, on the weirdness scale he's about an eleven. Supposedly some scary shit happened to him when he was a kid. Messed up his head. He's harmless, though. Probably just lonely.

Tim leans forward, ravaging Beth's neck.

TIM
Or horny.

KARA
Tim, do you always have to act like such an asshole?

TIM
Only when you're around to dump on ... Hey, chill, sis. I'm just doggin' ya.

Suddenly the van ROARS by and cuts them off. Beth lays on the HORN. Slams on the brakes. Narrowly avoiding a collision.

BETH
Speed kills, asshole!

Suddenly the van swerves around to face the VW head on. For a breathless moment the van and the VW sit at opposite ends of the intersection. Idling. A tense stand off.

KARA
Who is that ...

Kara strains to get a look at the van's driver. A momentary glimpse of a pale white face behind the wheel.

BETH
(bravely)
I've got my pepper spray.

Danny sits frozen in the back seat. Suddenly the van shoots forward, tires SCREAMING. Startled GASPS. The van turns off sharply at the last second, SCREECHING down the next block.

TIM
(relieved)
Happy fuckin' Halloween.

BETH
Someone's trying to scare us out of having this fair ... and it's not gonna work.

Beth drives on, grimly determined. Kara looks back at Danny. He returns her frightened gaze.

INT. TOMMY'S APARTMENT - DAY

Tommy paces in his cramped apartment. Dark circles under his eyes.
A remote control in hand, reviewing his recording of last night's
Harry Simms broadcast:

HARRY SIMMS (V.O.)
So they're trying to kill you and your baby. Don't tell me. Your name also happens to be Rosemary.

JAMIE (V.O.)
No, please listen! They're coming ... coming for me and my baby.

HARRY SIMMS (V.O.)
Come on, sweetheart what is this? Who's coming?

JAMIE (V.O.)
It's ... Michael ... Michael Myers!
Frustrated, Tommy plays it again. Adjusts the speed. Tries to make out something else in the b.g. Jamie's voice comes through. Slow.
Eerie.

JAMIE (V.O.)
(continuing; slowed)
It's ... Michael ... Michael Myers!
Another VOICE, distant and distorted, filters up behind hers.

ANNOUNCER (V.O.)
Bus 611 from Russellville now arriving.
Tommy quickly stops the tape, throws on his worn leather bomber jacket and bolts straight out the door.
MOVE IN on a pair of old newspaper clippings left on the floor.
Headlines read: "November 5, 1989. JAMIE LLOYD STILL MISSING."
"November 19, 1989. MYERS' NIECE PRESUMED DEAD."

DISSOLVE TO:
INT. FORD EXPLORER / EXT. RURAL HIGHWAY - MORNING
Tommy drives like a bat out of hell. The "Greyhound" sign looms ahead.

EXT. BUS DEPOT - MORNING (CONTINUOUS)
The Explorer pulls up to the depot. Tommy makes a beeline for the entrance, cowboy boots splashing through rain puddles.

INT. BUS DEPOT (CONTINUOUS)
Tommy wades his way through a small crowd up to the ticket booth. A cross eyed ATTENDANT greets him.

ATTENDANT
Can I help you, sir?

TOMMY
Can you tell me if a bus arrived from
Russellville last night?
The Attendant checks her roster.

ATTENDANT
Sure did. About seven hours ago. You lookin' for someone

TOMMY
(walking away)
Thank you.
The Attendant eyes Tommy suspiciously as he enters the phone booth in the corner. Inside, he picks up the receiver and pretends to dial a number. Makes a cursory inspection.

TOMMY'S P.O.V. - PHONE BOOTH
On the floor, tiny droplets of what appear to be blood form a dotted trail out the door.

TOMMY follows the crimson path around the corner down a dim hallway, stopping at the door marked "Ladies Room." Checking first to make sure the coast is clear, he steps furtively inside.

INT. LADIES' ROOM (CONTINUOUS)
Tommy walks past the sink. Water drips into the filthy basin. He touches something inside, rubs it on his fingers blood.
Tommy whirls, startled by a sudden NOISE. Muffled, indistinct.
Like CRYING. Tommy gathers his courage as he slowly moves past the long row of empty stalls. The CRIES grow louder as he reaches the final stall. Jamie's escape route the window still wide open.
A hole in the wall behind the toilet. Tommy reaches in, his hands locking onto something. Shock and amazement overcome him when he lifts out a baby Jamie's baby.

TOMMY
Jesus ...
The helpless newborn kicks and CRIES, the triangular symbol of Thorn still caked in blood over his tiny torso.

SUBJECTIVE P.O.V.
Someone partially opens the door, peering in from the hallway as
Tommy removes his jacket and bundles the baby inside.

TOMMY
Okay, little guy. You're okay.

BACK TO SCENE
A CREAK. Tommy looks up. The door slowly closes.

DEPOT HALLWAY
Tommy looks into shadowy stillness. No one there. Hiding the baby, cradling his jacket, he hurries through the crowd and slinks out the door marked ENTRANCE.

SHOCK
HELICOPTER P.O.V.
The SOUND of THWACKING BLADES as we FLY past a winding rural highway over a dense grove of oak trees massive, ancient guardians of the sprawling pumpkin patch that lies beyond.
As we circle the field, red and blue gum machines police cars, fire engines and ambulances can be seen through gauzy veils of rising BLACK SMOKE, dissipating with the strong WIND.
Charred in the ground, three intersecting lines stretch a hundred feet across the plan to form a vivid geoglyphic. The symbol of
Thorn.

HELICOPTER PILOT (V.O.)
(filtered)
Chopper One to Smith's Grove. We've got a visual. Approximately ten miles due east of
Haddonfield.

INT. HELICOPTER (CONTINUOUS)
Loomis surveys the crash site with morbid fascination. Wynn, wearing headphones, shouts over the noise.

WYNN
(pointing)
What is that?

LOOMIS
It's a sign. He's come home.

EXT. PUMPKIN PATCH - MORNING (CONTINUOUS)
The helicopter lands, windmilling gusts of ashen earth. Loomis and
Wynn jump out, ducking past the spinning blades.
We FOLLOW them through EMERGENCY CREWS and a few CURIOSITY SEEKERS toward the center of attention. A charred body is lifted from the eviscerated, flame blackened pikcup truck.
A few feet away, a team of PARAMEDICS work frantically around another body, hidden among a cluster of pumpkins.
Loomis surges forward, at once halted by an armed DEPUTY.

DEPUTY
Sir, you'll have to step back.

LOOMIS
Please. I need to see the sheriff.

WYNN
Official business.
Wynn flashes his badge. The Deputy gives them a vexed glance.

DEPUTY
Wait here.
Loomis's eyes flicker with nervous anticipation. The Deputy whispers something to SHERIFF JIM HOLDT, a brooding giant of a man who dons a Stetson, holstered .44 Special and steel toed boots that give new meaning to the term "bad ass."
Even Loomis steps back as the sheriff lumbers toward them.

LOOMIS
(extends his hand)
You must be Sheriff Holdt.
Holdt responds by stubbing out his Marlboro at Loomis's foot.

HOLDT
As a matter of fact, I am. And I take it you're the infamous Dr. Loomis.

LOOMIS
I'd like to introduce you to Terence Wynn, the
Chief of Staff at

HOLDT
Smith's Grove. They told me you'd be coming.
Now I suggest you fly right on back to your crackpot asylum. You people got no business in my town.

LOOMIS
Michael Myers is my business.
Holdt towers above him.

HOLDT
I want you to listen and listen good, Loomis.
Things have been quiet for six years and that's the way they're gonna stay. The last thing we need is you spouting off your ghost stories.
As usual, Loomis isn't easily intimidated.

LOOMIS
I suppose it was a ghost that did all this. A ghost who called the radio station last night. Maybe that same ghost is lying over there right now.
Holdt fumes, ready to boil when

DEPUTY
Sheriff! She's alive!

Holdt and Loomis wade through the crush of paramedics, running alongside the stretcher being whisked toward an ambulance.

A large knife extruding from a girl's stomach, packed under sterile gauze. Skin pasty white. Lips blue from shock.

LOOMIS
Dear God ... Jamie!

EXT. HADDONFIELD JUNIOR COLLEGE - PARKING LOT - MORNING

Beth's car pulls into the parking lot of a picturesque, impeccably landscaped campus, speckled with colorful leaves. A buzz of excitement fills the autumn air.

Tim and Beth are surprised to see a small crowd camped out in sleeping bags, holding "We Love to Hate Harry" signs.

TIM
Yo, check it out. They've been lining up all night just to see Harry.
(to Kara)
You lose your mind in that thing, Kara?

Kara is nervously rifling through her enormous book bag.

KARA
I can't find my term paper.

TIM
So copy someone else's. I do it all the time.
Works primo.

Armed with her clipboard, Beth is assailed by her COMMITTEE. Inundating her with QUESTIONS.

BETH
Give us victory or give us death. See you tonight, Kara!

Tim and Beth are swept away. A large sheet of paper falls out of Kara's bag. She picks it up, startled by what she sees.

KARA'S P.O.V. - THE DRAWING

Crayola figures of Grandma, Grandpa, Uncle Tim, and Mommy. Knives piercing them. Blood dripping. Mouths screaming. A black shadow figure bearing the word "THORN." On the flip side, the drawing she found last night. Danny's scribbling of the odd triangular symbol.

BACK TO SCENE

The horrifying images send chills up Kara's spine.

KARA

Thorn ...

Lost in grim reverie, Kara walks on, oblivious to the activity all around her ...

A banner hangs from the eaves of the library: "HADDONFIELD JR.

COLLEGE - FIRST ANNUAL HARVEST FAIRE."

Tim and Beth supervise as preparations for tonight's event get underway.
STUDENT VOLUNTEERS nailing together booths, hanging decorations. A half assembled Ferris wheel, a merry go round, an ominous looking
House of Horrors.
Rounding the corner onto the quiet path behind the library, Kara suddenly finds herself alone. WIND whips at her hair. She glances over her shoulder, as if sensing a presence.

KARA'S P.O.V.

No one is there. Just the rustling of leaves on the ground.

ANGLE ON KARA

Walking off in the distance. Suddenly the Shape steps shockingly into FRAME, watching her disappear around the corner.

SHOCK

INT. HADDONFIELD MEMORIAL - EMERGENCY ROOM - DAY

Doors BLAST open. The stretcher holding Jamie is pushed through,
Loomis right beside her. Wynn follows, trying to stop him. A
SHOCK TRAUMA unit swarms in. No time to lose.

PARAMEDIC

Penetrating abdominal trauma. Massive blood loss. We've given her two units of O negative stat and dextran. BP sixty. Pulse one twenty
... Somehow she pulled through out there all night!
DR. BONHAM, the ER resident, peels off the sheet, exposing a dark sea of blood around the enormous knife still jutting from Jamie's stomach. Bonham stares, incredulous.

DR. BONHAM

How can this girl still be alive?! Type and cross match for another six units! Get a CT scan and move her into surgery.
(re Loomis and Wynn)
And get them out of here!
ORDERLIES move in. Loomis won't release Jamie's hand.

WYNN

Sam, don't let them take care of her.

LOOMIS

I'm here now, Jamie. You're going to live.

You have to.

HOSPITAL ENTRANCE / ADMITTANCE DESK
Pneumatic doors fly open. Tommy bursts through, holding the baby in his jacket. PATIENTS and COPS everywhere. He hones in on the NURSE behind the admittance desk.

TOMMY
I need to see a doctor.

NURSE
What seems to be the problem?

TOMMY
I it's a baby my baby. There's been been an accident.

NURSE
What kind of an accident?

TOMMY
(explodes)
Just get me a doctor right now!

ADJACENT HALLWAY
Wynn and Loomis skirt past a line of SECURITY GUARDS.

WYNN
There's nothing more you can do for her.
The shrill sound of Wynn's beeper. He clicks it.

WYNN
(continuing)
I'll be right back.
Wynn disappears around the corner. Loomis wanders off alone.

TOMMY (O.S.)
Dr. Loomis!
Loomis reacts, taken aback by the frantic young man bounding toward him.

LOOMIS
Yes?

TOMMY
Dr. Loomis, thank God you're here. You heard her, didn't you? It was Jamie.

LOOMIS

35

I'm sorry, but do I know you

TOMMY
I'm Tommy. Tommy Doyle. Laurie Strode
Jamie's mother she was baby sitting for me that night
Loomis suddenly recognizes him. It's been a very long time.

LOOMIS
Yes ... Tommy. What are you doing here?

TOMMY
Please just tell me the truth. Has Michael
Myers come home?
Loomis pulls Tommy aside into an empty alcove.

LOOMIS
What do you know about Michael?

TOMMY
I know he's alive. People in this town they want us to believe he's dead. But I know. I've always known.

LOOMIS
Right now at least one girl is dead and Jamie
Lloyd is in there fighting for her life. She is the last of his blood line. If she dies

TOMMY
(gravely)
No, Dr. Loomis. She's not the last night.
Tommy hesitates. Loomis's eyes are drawn enigmatically to the infant in Tommy's arms.

TOMMY
(continuing; startled realization)
Oh, God his cousins. The Strodes. They're living in the Myers house!
Loomis's face flls with horror. Tommy sees the Admittance Nurse, flanked by a pair of security guards, walking his way.

TOMMY
(continuing)
I gotta go.
Tommy bolts toward the exit. Loomis tries to stop him.

LOOMIS
Tommy, wait!
But he is gone. A hand taps Loomis's shoulder; he reels. Wynn.

WYNN
There you are. Who was that boy?

LOOMIS
An old friend.
Darkness fills Loomis's countenance as we

EXT. MYERS HOUSE - DAY
We peer OVER THE SHOULDER of the Shape, standing across the street.
Watching Debra, in jeans and a rumpled sweatshirt, collecting left over painting supplies from the front porch.
Debra starts to open the CREAKY screen door when she notices the axe
John had used earlier. Clumsily picks it up and slides it through the top of the crate she is holding.

INT. MYERS HOUSE - FOYER (CONTINUOUS)
Laden with her heavy load, Debra nudges the door shut with her foot. Then crosses to another door the cellar door.

INT. MYERS HOUSE - CELLAR - DAY (CONTINUOUS)
Debra, silhouetted at the top of the stairs, hits a light switch; a naked bulb springs to life. Slowly she descends the rickety staircase.
The basement, pitch dark save for a spear of sunlight shooting through an elevated window, is overrun with cobwebs, rusted tools and broken bicycle parts. A clunker of a washing machine RATTLES in the corner.
Debra makes space for the crate in a storage cabinet. Suddenly the washing machine stops. Nonplissed, she moves toward it. Lifts the lid. The bed sheets inside are sopping wet.
Opening the electrical fuse box, she flicks a switch back and forth a few times but the washing machine doesn't respond.

DEBRA
Great.
Frustrated, Debra looks down to see a large puddle of water forming on the floor.

INT. MYERS HOUSE - FOYER (SAME)
Debra hauls a laundry basket upstairs, filled with wet sheets. She turns, startled. The front door is standing wide open.
Just as she goes to shut it, a man steps out from the living room behind her. She gasps, dropping the basket; it's Loomis.

LOOMIS
I'm very sorry, Mrs. Strode.
Debra shudders at the sight of the beguiling, wide eyed man.

LOOMIS

(continuing)
I've been knocking. The door was open. Is everything all right in here?

DEBRA
(defensively)
Who are you?

LOOMIS
I've come to help your family.
Debra steps aside as Loomis walks in right past her. Holding a valuminous file bearing the name "MICHAEL AUDREY MYERS."

INT. TOMMY'S APARTMENT - DAY
The SOUND of JANGLING KEYS. A door UNLOCKING. Tommy scrambles in, the baby iin one arm, a bag of groceries under the other.
With a single swipe, he clears away the junk on his futin, then carefully lays down the CRYING infant. He digs through the bag:
Baby Wipes. Diapers. Formula. Bottles.

TOMMY
Shhh. Okay, okay, Kyle. You like that name?
Yeah, I think it suits you.
Quickly he scans the directions on the formula. Pours the liquid into a bottle, nukes it in the microwave, then returns to the business at hand.
Tommy grimaces at the mess inside his leather bomber. The baby
CRIES harder.

TOMMY
(continuing)
This is worse for me than it is for you.
Armed with Baby Wipe and a diaper, Tommy goes to work.

UPSTAIRS HALLWAY (SAME)
Mrs. Blankenship traverses the hall outside Tommy's apartment. The baby's CRIES; Tommy's GROSSED OUT GROANS can clearly be heard. But the old woman keeps walking, oblivious to it all.

TOMMY'S APARTMENT (SAME)
Tommy finishes securing the diaper. The baby in his arms, he tests the formula's temperature and feeds him. The infant sucks voraciously. The crying stops. Tommy rocks him gently.

TOMMY
It's okay, big guy. Don't you worry. I'm gonna take care of you.

INT. MYERS HOUSE - LIVING ROOM (SAME)

Loomis, setting out the case file on Michael Myers gruesome photographs of the murder scenes has Debra's undivided attention.

LOOMIS
Michael Myers was just six years old when he stabbed his sister to death in 1963. Here in this house. For the next fifteen years, I became obsessed with finding out what was living inside of him. He was my lift's work and my ultimate failure. I knew what he was but I never knew why.

INT. COLLEGE CLASSROOM (SAME)
Kara sits in the front row of a classrooom as a PROFESSOR drones on. He looks at Kara, something frightening in his gaze. Watching as her pen glides dreamily over her notebook.

LOOMIS (V.O.)
There's a living force inside of him. Driving him. And I fear that somehow it has been unleashed again.

KARA'S P.O.V. - NOTEBOOK
An entire page of scribbled triangles. The mark of Thorn.

EXT. ELEMENTARY SCHOOL - PLAYGROUND - DAY
A group of KIDS engaged in a game of Pogs two opponents facing off, slamming down the colored discs. Lunch money on the ground.
High stakes indeed.
IAN, a lunkish 5th grader, is clearly the man to be reckoned with.

IAN
Who's my next victim?
The other kids make way as Danny takes the empty spot on the tetherball court, sitting face to face with the inplacable Ian.
Danny says nothign as he places his bet and slams the stack of
Pogs. Ian glowers. Easy money. The showdown begins.

INT. MYERS HOUSE - HALLWAY / KARA'S ROOM
Loomis vivdly reenacts the nightmare as Debra shows him upstairs.

LOOMIS
He crept up these stairs and made his way into this room. His sister's room. Right here. Where it all began.

DEBRA
(near tears)
What makes you think he'll come here again?

LOOMIS

This house is sacred to him. It's the source of his memories his rage. Mrs. Strode, I beg you. Don't let your family suffer the same fast as Laurie and her daughter.

DEBRA
Jamie? But I thought she was

LOOMIS
Found this morning. In a field outside Haddonfield. Stabbed.

INT. HOSPITAL - OPERATING ROOM - DAY
Dr. Bonham and his team surround Jamie, anesthetized on the operating table, her condition weak but stable.
Blood flows from the gaping wound in her abdomen. Slowly, painstakingly, the knife is extracted.
A NURSE takes a sample of a thick, viscous fluid from beneath
Jamie's gown and holds it up to the light for the doctor.

EXT. PLAYGROUND - DAY (SAME)
Danny wins another round. His till growing. More kids gather to watch. Ian is losing his cool, determined to save face.

IAN
Double or nothing.
Danny pushes over the stack, nothing incisive in his manner. Ian retorts, angrily slamming his Pogs.

IAN
(continuing)
Look how he sits there. Little freak. Just like the bogeyman who used to live in his house. Are you the bogeyman, Danny?
Ian trumps Danny's hand and smiles haughtily. The low, whispering
VOICE which only Danny can hear RUMBLES in his mind.

WHISPERING VOICE (V.O.)
Kill him, Danny ... Kill him now ...
Danny stares blankly across the playground.

DANNY'S P.O.V.
The white van is parked across the street. A tall figure in black stands beside it, watching Danny. The Stranger!

INT. CAMPUS LIBRARY - DAY
Kara sits glued behind a computer monitor, the glow of the screen reflected in her reading glasses.

LOOMIS (V.O.)
This force which drives him, which keeps him alive, comes from something more powerful more deadly than we can possibly imagine. The embodiment of all that is evil.

KARA'S P.O.V.
A litany of topics scroll up the screen. Kara punches in one of them. Card catalog entry reads: "Thorn: The Devil's Rune."

EXT. PLAYGROUND (SAME)
Spellbound, Danny slams down the winning Pog. Methodically, he dumps the money in his Halloween bag and begins to walk away.
Ian sees red. Written across Danny's last Pog: "DIE, FAT ASS."

IAN
You crazy little freak!!!
Ian goes berserk, leaping out at Danny like an enraged lion. The kids cheer him on as a full fledged playground brawl ensues.
Danny breaks away. Runs. With an amazing burst of strength, he swings a tetherball. Th ball CRACKS Ian right between his eyes, laying the bully flat on his ass.

INT. MYERS HOUSE (SAME)
Debra leads Loomis to the front door, her face clouded with fear.

DEBRA
What should I do?

LOOMIS
Lock the doors and call your husband. Get your family as far away from Haddonfield as possible.

DEBRA
God ... this can't be true.

LOOMIS
Mrs. Strode, Michael Myers is here to kill his family. And he won't stop until you are all destroyed. I only thank God that I found you before he did.
Loomis grips her hand reassuringly, then heads out the door. Debra turns the deadbolt, securing it with the chain lock. She collapses against the wall, tears of horror in her eyes.

EXT. PLAYGROUND / GATE (SAME)
A TEACHER blows a WHISTLE, wading through the screaming, cheering kids as Danny pummels Ian brutally with his fist.
The teacher helps Ian out of the fray, eyes warbling, nose and mouth bleeding. Danny takes off running toward the gate.

Suddenly he barrels into the outstretched hands of a towering shape. Danny looks up in shock at a stone faced man Tommy!

INT. CAMPUS LIBRARY - DAY
MOVING with Kara through long rows of books a veritable labyrinth of knowledge. She comes down a deserted aisle, searching. Her eyes spotting what she is looking for. She pulls out an old, dusty tome and begins flipping through its pages.
As she reads we SEE the cover: "Runes and Ancient Black Magic."

EXT. STRODE REALTY - DAY
ESTABLISHING. A modest, one story building located in the older business section of town. Cheap Halloween decorations hang in the windows. An "OPEN" sign on the front door.
MOANS of ecstasy resound along the street, attracting the attention of the mid day passerby.

HARRY SIMMS (V.O.)
I'm coming. Yes. I'm coming. Get ready. I'm coming. Oh, yes! Yesss!!!
The WKNB station van rolls by; another Harry Simms plug. Some people laugh. Others wince in disgust.

HARRY SIMMS (V.O.)
(continuing)
Made ya look!!! I'm coming, all right. And you better be there. Tonight. Let's do it together.

INT. STRODE REALTY - DAY (CONTINUOUS)
A sparesely furnished office screaming for renovation. Business is obviously slow. John rattles a jammed file cabinet, then kicks it in a fit of angry frustration before answering the incessantly
RINGING phone.

JOHN
(barking)
Strode Realty.

INT. MYERS HOUSE - KITCHEN
Debra on the other end. Tears reddening her cheeks.

DEBRA
John, it's me. Something terrible has happened.
INTERCUT their conversation.

JOHN
What is it this time?

DEBRA
A man came by the house. A psychiatrist by the name of Loomis.
John stiffens, slowly sits down behind his desk.

DEBRA
(continuing)
He told me about the terrible things that happened here. In our house.

JOHN
What the fuck are you doing letting strangers in without

DEBRA
(releasing)
John, they sound Jamie Lloyd this morning!
Someone tried to kill her!

JOHN
What in God's name are you talking about, woman? When are you gonna stop listening to those damned talk shows?

DEBRA
I'm getting the children out of here. At least until we know what we're dealing with.
John, I want you to come with us.

JOHN
(whispers)
Debra, you're fuckin' insane.

DEBRA
You knew, didn't you, John? You knew.
A CLICK as the line suddenly goes DEAD.
John scowls, opens his lower desk drawer, produces a bottle of JD and a small glass.
He blows off dust and begins to pour.

JOHN
Trick or treat to you, too.

INT. MYERS HOUSE - UPSTAIRS (SAME)
CAMERA FOLLOWS Debra in frantic flight from bedroom to bedroom, throwing open closets and drawers, filling a suitcase with a night's worth of clothes for her family. She accidentally knocks a family portrait off a bureau. Glass SHATTERS.

FOYER / LIVING ROOM
Debra drags the suitcase downstairs. Lets out a horrified gasp.
The crate she had previously stored in the cellar is now sitting in the center of the hallway ...

The axe that had been sticking out of it earlier is now missing!
The telephone RINGS. Eyes riveted to the crate, Debra backs away down the hall. Into the living room. Picks up the phone.

DEBRA
Hello?
A startling, intensely whispering VOICE:

WHISPERING VOICE (V.O.)
We want the child ...
Debra slams down the phone. Terror paralyzing her.
MUFFLED, HEAVY BREATHING fills the room.

DEBRA
Oh, God ...
Debra races back into the foyer and struggles with the door. In her panic, she can't release the chain lock.
She turns to see the Shape standing right behind her! Debra
SCREAMS. Breaks for the hall. Through the kitchen. Flings open the back door.

EXT. BACK YARD - DAY (CONTINUOUS)
Debra half runs, half stumbles through the endless rows of clotheslines. White sheets twist around her like ghosts in the blustering WIND. She tosses them aside, one after the other.
Approaching the driveway. Safety up ahead.
Whipping aside the last sheet, Debra finds herself staring into the
Shape's death mask. Her eyes bug. Too late to scream. The missing axe swings at her like a sledge hammer. Blood paints the sheets red as we

DISSOLVE TO:
EXT. COLLEGE CAMPUS - DUSK
Laden with her book bag, Kara exits the library and heads across the campus green. All around her, the sights and sounds of the impending carnival come to life.
Rides assembled. Paper witches hang from broomsticks. Goblins lurk behind syrofoam gravestones.
Kara waves at Beth in the distance, making last minute preparations. Student volunteers scurrying in every which direction. Donning costumes.
A ducking for apples booth. Homebaked goodies set out on picnic tables. Long rows of pumpkins lined up for a jack o' lantern carving contest.
The centerpiece of all this is a huge, magnificently decorated
HALLOWEEN TREE. Tim and a gaggle of WORKERS stream up ladders, stringing lights, hoisting up colorful bunting filled with mounds of candy.
As Kara walks along, her hair being tossed about in the brisk WIND, she becomes aware of the magical, almost out of time quality that seems to hang in the air.

EXT. STREET (SAME)

Kara walks past the crows of "Harry ites" gathered outside the campus gates, now extending half way around the block.
The WKNB van rolls by, exhorting the crowd with the voice of the man they've all come to see:

HARRY SIMMS (V.O.)
It's almost that time, all you kiddies and women with big hey, what rhymes with kiddies? So let's count it down as we get down to the witching hour!
Kara walks on, smiling to herself as the crowd bursts into gales of wild, exuberant CHEERS.

EXT. LAMPKIN LANE / MYERS HOUSE - DUSK
The setting sun glows behind the trees, casting long shadows as Kara rounds the corner onto her street.
KIDS already pouring out of their homes, some accompanied by
PARENTS, others joining groups of friends.
Kara ambles up the walk of the Myers house, shoes clapping up the porch steps as she digs the keys out of her overstuffed bag.
Unbolting the door, she finds that it's secured with the chain lock. Kara pushes on it, calling inside.

KARA
Mom, I'm home ... Hello?
No response. Puzzled, she steps off the porch and makes her way around the side of the house, CAMERA FOLLOWING as she peers into the windows along the way.

BACK YARD (CONTINUOUS)
Kara walks along the billowing clotheslines, passing the blank spot where the blood stained sheets were and are no longer.
She reaches the back door. Standing ajar.

KARA
Mom?
Casting one last glance across the yard, she steps inside.

INT. MYERS HOUSE - KITCHEN (SAME)
Everything in its proper place. Kara drops her heavy bag on the kitchen table and proceeds down the hall.

LIVING ROOM / FOYER - DUSK INTO NIGHT (CONTINUOUS)
The room is quickly falling into darkness. The eeriness almost palpable. Kara advances into the living room, eyes roaming.

KARA
Mom? ... Danny?

Nothing. Kara moves into the foyer. Her mother's suitcase still sitting there. Beyond, the cellar door stands wide open. Kara moves toward it, peering into blackness.
A sudden CRASH from upstairs. Kara jerks the door closed and looks up the deeply shadowed staircase.

KARA
(continuing)
Mom? Are you there?
A muffled ROAR. Kara mounts the staircase.

UPSTAIRS HALLWAY (CONTINUOUS)
Kara reaches the second floor landing and moves slowly toward the door at the end of the hall. Danny's room. An orange glow flickers around the edges of the closed door.

KARA'S P.O.V.
Her hand grabs the doorknob, turns it. The door swings open.

DANNY'S BEDROOM
Someone sitting on the edge of Danny's bed. A man. His back turned. Dinosaurs ROAR on Sega Genesis. Danny squatting on the floor, engrossed in his game.
Kara stares at the intruder in horrified disbelief.

KARA
Who the hell are you?
The man watching over Danny turns toward Kara. It's Tommy.

TOMMY
I I'm your neighbor from across the street. My name's Tommy. Tommy Doyle.
Panicked, Kara makes a wall of herself between Tommy and Danny. The little boy isn't the least bit fazed.

KARA
What are you doing with my son? Where's my mother?
Tommy backs off a tick, calmly trying to explain.

TOMMY
She wasn't here when I brought Danny home from

KARA
(fortissimo)
Danny, go downstairs Now!
Danny finally looks up, exasperated.

DANNY
Tommy's my new friend. We've been playing 'til you got home. He knows all about dinosaurs.

One look at Danny's black eye and Kara goes ballistic.

KARA
My, God! What have you done to him?

TOMMY
I didn't He got in a fight and I

KARA
You stay away from him!
Kara starts to drag Danny away by the arm. He resists angrily.

DANNY
It wasn't Tommy! It was the voice man.
Kara sees Tommy hunkering down in the corner, lifting something out of a crate a makeship crib. He turns, his expression very grave. Holding the baby.

TOMMY
I want you to listen very carefully to everything I'm about to tell you.
Kara's face is a melange of wonder and fear as we

DISSOLVE TO:
INT. JAMIE'S HOSPITAL ROOM - NIGHT
Jamie lies comatose, ensconced in the dim GLOW of monitors.
Sustained by I.V.s and a breathing apparatus.
MOVE IN on Jamie. EKG registers rapid heartbeat. MOVE IN TIGHT on her eyes, darting beneath closed lids.

INT. CORRIDOR - DISTORTED VISION (DREAM SEQUENCE)
Blood chilling SCREAMS as we MOVE rapidly through a BLINDING TUNNEL
OF LIGHT. Blurred, indistinct images. FIGURES wearing long white coats flash along sterile walls.
As we BLAST around corners, we realize we are seeing from the P.O.V. of a girl being pushed forward on a gurney. It is Jamie.
Her arm injected with a sedative. Eyes lolling. Succumbing.

JAMIE'S P.O.V. - MOVING (DREAM SEQUENCE)
Even more DISTORTED now, images swirling at random. Cold, staring
FACES. Flashing lights on a wall panel: "3 2 1 B" an elevator.
Going down. Down. Beneath the basement level.
The doors open. The gurney SLAMS out into DARKNESS. VOICES ECHO.
Lighted torches flicker on craggy walls.

JAMIE (O.S.)
Please don't let him do this to me.

VOICE (O.S.)
We're not going to hurt you, Jamie. He chose you. Now it's time.

SHAPE'S P.O.V.
Pacing back and forth behind iron bars, agitated, disturbed. SEEING Jamie strapped to a table. Surrounded by robed figures. CHANTING.
Weakly, Jamie reaches out toward the cell.

JAMIE
Please, Michael ... Help me.
Suddenly a long SHADOW fills the room. The P.O.V. becomes more restless as the Stranger glides toward Jamie and disrobes. The figures close the circle. Jamie SCREAMS in terror.
The Shape's hands SLAM violently against the iron bars, a horrific
SHUDDER of metal as we

SHOCK
INT. JAMIE'S HOSPITAL ROOM - NIGHT (SAME)
Jamie's eyes flash open! A dark shadow fills the room. The Stranger descends on her!
Gloved hand covers Jamie's mouth. A switchblade FLICKS open.

WHISPERING VOICE (O.S.)
Your work is done, Jamie.
The glinting blade SLASHES across Jamie's throat, cutting off her soundless scream!
Then the Stranger flows out of the room. Spurs CLANKING. Like a thief in the night.
The shrill sound of a BEEPER going off as we

SLOW DISSOLVE TO:
EXT. HADDONFIELD STREETS - NIGHT - SERIES OF SHOTS
The dark blanket of night envelops the little town. The LIGHTS of the fair twinkle in the distance, bright and beckoning.
Families men, women and children alike turn out from their homes wearing COSTUMES, joining a growing procession along the peaceful streets of Haddonfield.
A large group of PROTESTORS carry PICKET SIGNS in front of the campus gates. Rallying against the celebration.
Haddonfield's finest out in full force, squad cars sweeping alongside a black STRETCH LIMO as it makes its way through town.
Tinted windows make it impossible to see inside.

EXT. CAMPUS PARKING LOT / HARVEST FAIR ENTRANCE - NIGHT
Tim and Beth, standouts as punk versions of Frankenstein and his bride, stride purposefully toward the fair entrance. Beth is a jumble of nerves as she runs down her checklist of events.

BETH

Seven thirty is the costume pageant ... Carving jack o' lanterns at eight ... Photos for the school paper at nine ... Then Harry lights the tree at nine thirty ... I just know I'm forgetting something!

TIM
Relax. Everything's cool. Didn't I tell you
Harry would be here?
The limo crawls into the parking lot. A stampede of overzealous
FANS surge past them.

BETH
That's what worries me.
Tim and Beth move into the fair, with all its noise and colorful movement.

ANOTHER ANGLE
KIDS waving signs and T shirts. Throwing themselves at the windows. Frenzied CLAMORING. Harry mania abound.
The WKNB van parks parallel to the steps of the library, adorned with HAREM GIRLS and a large golden throne. The side door opens. A red carpet is rolled out.
A tall, imposing figure emerges from the van and walks up the steps. Spurs CLANKING on black boots. "Jesse James" style duster.
Hat cocked slightly.

HARRY SIMMS (V.O.)
Hellllo, Haddonfield!!!
The crowd turns in a mass of confusion. Standing above them, waving from a microphone, is HARRY. Dark sunglasses. Gaunt, glacial features and an outrageous mane of black hair.
Suddenly Harry throws open his duster flashing them revealing that he has nothing on beneath except his boots and a pair of bright orange boxer shorts that say "HAPPY HALLOWEEN."
The kids go insane.

ANGLE ON LOOMIS
Making his way through the teeming crowd. Walkie talkie in hand.
The helicopter zooms overhead. Wynn's voice squawks over garbled
RADIO CHATTER. Conducting a surveillance by air.

WYNN (V.O.)
(filtered)
There's more people moving eastbound down Old
Reservoir Road past the elementary school.

LOOMIS
(into walkie talkie)
Any word on the location of the Strodes?

WYNN (V.O.)
No one's home. Checked it out myself.

LOOMIS
Good. I want around the clock surveillance on that house.
Suddenly Loomis is waylaid by a giant wall of a man Sheriff Holdt. Loomis meets his fiery gaze.

HOLDT
I'm warning you, Loomis stay out of my way.
You may have had free reign when Ben Meeker was sheriff, God rest his soul, but I'm in charge now. And I'm not about to stand by and watch you turn this night into some kind of sadistic witch hunt.

WYNN (V.O.)
Sam, I just got word from the hospital. You'd better get over there right away.

LOOMIS
(into walkie talkie)
What's wrong? What's happened to Jamie?

WYNN (V.O.)
I'll meet you over there.
Loomis tears off. Holdt stares brazenly, throwing down his cigarette. Crushes it under his boot and slowly follows him.

INT. BLANKENSHIP HOUSE - LOBBY - NIGHT
Carrying the CRYING baby, Tommy leads Kara and Danny into the lobby of the vintage boarding home. Polished wood. Framed old paintings. Wall to wall Tiffany lamps.
Mrs. Blankenship sits behind the front desk, oblivious to the
GRINDING and SCREAMING on the television as "The Texas Chain Saw Massacre" reaches its horrific climax on the annual Horrorthon.

TOMMY
Quiet around here tonight, huh, Mrs. B.?
As usual, the senile old woman doesn't reply.

KARA
(indignantly; to Tommy)
Do you mind telling me what this is all about?
Tim and Beth are waiting for us.
Tommy ushers Kara and Danny up the stairs. Mrs. Blankenship stares at the boy the kind of stare that would send most kids running for their moms. But Danny is undaunted.

INT. TOMMY'S APARTMENT (CONTINUOUS)
The door opens. Kara is repulsed by the sight of Tommy's musty, unkempt apartment.

DANNY
Mom, I want to go to the fair ...

KARA
(to Tommy)
You can't expect us to stay here
Tommy adjusts the blinds on the window looking out on the Myers house.

TOMMY
I want you to watch your house. You can see everything from this window.
Kara glares, reminded of last night.

KARA
Do you know how insane this is? Who am I supposed to be looking for?

TOMMY
Him.
Tommy flashes a newspaper article in front of her. One we've seen eariler: "MICHAEL MYERS DEAD OF ALIVE?"
The baby's SCREAMS are verging on overload. Tommy dashes to the recessed kitchen area and heats up another bottle.
As Kara reads, Danny tugs at his mother's blouse.

DANNY
Come on, Mom. We're gonna miss all the fun stuff!

KARA
(snapping)
Danny, you're just going to have to wait!
Danny plods off. Kara hands Tommy a nipple for the bottle. Their eyes lock for a beat. He takes it.

TOMMY
Shhh. It's okay, Kyle. Just give me one more
(the microwave BEEPS)
second. There you go, big guy.
Kara looks on as Tommy attempts to feed the baby. Despite his clumsiness, she's undeniably moved.
Behind them, Danny's imagination kicks into high gear as he drives a
Power Ranger over an invisible race track. On the floor. Across the windowsill. Glancing across the street.

DANNY'S P.O.V. - THE MYERS HOUSE

Standing below on the front lawn is the Shape, silhouetted under a moonlit tree. Looking right at Danny.

BACK TO SCENE

Danny backs away, terrified. Tommy and Kara are too concerned with the baby to notice.

TOMMY
God, what's wrong with him?

KARA
Here. Let me try.
Tommy gingerly hands the baby over to her. Instantaneously, Kyle's CRIES subside.

KARA
(continuing; fawning)
There. All it takes is a mother's touch.
For one fleeting moment, Tommy and Kara find themselves smiling at one another. Unaware as Danny glides silently out the door.
Tommy's expression darkens once again. A man possessed.

TOMMY
Kyle's mother might be dead for all I know.
Now I'm afraid he could be next.

KARA
Why would anyone want to kill an innocent baby?

TOMMY
Not just Kyle. All of you. His entire family.
(reaching toward Kyle)
Here. Look at this.
Tommy opens the baby's quilt, revealing the blood mark smeared over his torso. Kara's face registers terrified recognition.

TOMMY
(continuing)
It was there when I found him this morning. It looks like some kind of letter or number or

KARA
It's a rune ... Thorn.

INT. JAMIE'S HOSPITAL ROOM / HALLWAY - NIGHT

POLICE on the scene. A crying NURSE gives a statement. A CRIME
SCENE PHOTOGRAPHER snapps photographs as Jamie's bloody corpse is covered over with a white sheet.
Loomis stands frozen in horror. Tears in his eyes.

LOOMIS
Jamie ... I failed you again. I never should have left you.
He spins, pouncing on Sheriff Holdt.

LOOMIS
(continuing)
Now will you do something?! How many more innocent people have to die?!
Wynn restrains him. Pulls him away. The sheriff doesn't budge.

WYNN
Don't do this to yourself, Sam. Let's go.
Come on.
Wynn ushers Loomis out of the room. Holdt stares apathetically.

HALLWAY (CONTINUOUS)
Wynn tries to calm Loomis down. Jamie's doctor approaches.

DR. BONHAM
Dr. Loomis?

WYNN
What is it?

DR. BONHAM
I'm very sorry ...

LOOMIS
You let it get to her. How could you?

DR. BONHAM
Dr. Loomis, there's something else you should know. During surgery, we discovered that
Jamie's uterus was hemorrhaging. We found this.
(displays a small vital)
It's placental fluid.

LOOMIS
God in heaven. You don't tell me she was

DR. BONHAM
I estimate she gave birth no more than a few hours before the attack.

WYNN
Then where's her baby?
Jamie's covered body is wheeled out past them. Loomis regards Wynn with a look of abject fear.

LOOMIS
I think I may already know ...

INT. TOMMY'S APARTMENT (SAME)
CLOSE ON a chapter heading. "Thorn The Devil's Rune." Beneath it, a bold depiction of the familiar Thorn triangle.
PULL BACK to REVEAL Tommy poring over the old library book. Kara paces, rocking the baby, feeding him with the bottle.

KARA
Runes were a kind of early alphabet that originated in Northern Europe thousands of years ago. They were symbols carved out of stone or pieces of wood. Of all the runes, Thorn had the most negative influence. Cults used them in blood rituals to portend future events and invoke magic.

TOMMY
Black magic ...
(reads)
'In ancient times, Thorn was believed to cause sickness, famine and death. Translated literally, it was the name of a demon spirit that delivered human sacrifices ... on the Celtic celebration of Samhain.'

KARA
Halloween.

TOMMY
'When applied directly to another person, Thorn could be used to call upon them confusion and destruction to literally visit them with the
Devil.'
Tommy jumps up, frantically moving around the apartment, collecting his jacket, his keys a gun.

KARA
(terrified)
Where are you going?

TOMMY
To find the rest of your family before Michael
Myers does or whoever's been controlling him.

An ominous CLICK as Tommy loads a cartridge into his gun. He bolts toward the door. Finds it standing wide open. Kara freezes, noticing for the first time that Danny is missing.

KARA
Oh, God Where's Danny? Kara flies down the hall, the baby in her arms. Tommy moves out right behind her.

INT. BLANKENSHIP HOUSE - LOBBY (CONTINUOUS)
Kara and Tommy barrel downstairs, searching frantically.

KARA
Danny?! Danny!

TOMMY
Mrs. Blankenship, have you seen the little boy who came in with me and
They find Mrs. Blankenship and Danny sitting side by side, watching the Horrorthon. A bowl of popcorn between them.

KARA
(grabs him)
Danny, don't ever walk off without telling me where you're going!
Danny looks at her. A blank, hollow stare. The old woman's eyes glitter madly.

MRS. BLANKENSHIP
The voice. He hears the voice. Just like the other little boy who used to live in that house.
Tommy throws on his jacket and opens the front door.

TOMMY
Take the kids upstairs, lock the door and wait for me.
(beat)
And Kara, whatever you do don't go back to your house.
Kara watches fearfully as Tommy heads out the door. Leaving her alone with the children.

EXT. HOUSES / STREET - NIGHT
Wind MOANS. Dead leaves blow across the WINDY lane as Tommy flies down the path of the Blankenship house and hops into his Explorer.
The Shape suddenly RISES INTO FRAME. Watching him peel off down the block. Taillights disappearing.
A moment later, another car rambles up the street, swerving erratically into the driveway of the Myers house.
The Shape watches.

INT. GARAGE - NIGHT (CONTINUOUS)

The car parks. Sits in silence. Suddenly the driver's side door opens, emblazoned with the "Strode Realty" emblem.

John spills out, collar unbuttoned, tie dangling. Picking himself up, he staggers out of the garage. Laughing. Singing.

JOHN
... Pretty woman, walking down the street ...
Pretty woman, the kind I'd like to meet.

EXT. MYERS HOUSE (CONTINUOUS)

FOLLOW John's circuitous route across the front lawn, stumbling over one of Danny's toys on his way up the porch steps.

JOHN
Damn kid ... this is my house ...

John fumbles wth his key, estimates the location of the lock. He turns the knob but the door's jammed. Chain locked.

JOHN
(continuing)
What the fuck ...
(yelling inside)
... Debra, open this goddamn door before I break it down! You got to three ...
(no response)
... One ... Two ...
(still no response)
... Two and a half ...

John slams his weight against the door. It doesn't budge.

Grumbling, John totters off the porch, trying to hold himself steady. Skirting along the side of the house.

INT. MYERS HOUSE - KITCHEN (CONTINUOUS)

John sways in through the back door and flicks on a light. Strains for lucidity. No one in the kitchen.

JOHN
Debra I'm home!

No answer. John shrugs and moves to the stove. Opens the lid on a pasta cooker. Nothing inside.

JOHN
(continuing; mutters)
Work all day and not even any supper ...

Frustrated, John opens the freezer and removes a frozen dinner.

Tears open the box and pops it in the microwave. Then he flounders down the dark alley, knocking picture frames awry.

LIVING ROOM / FOYER
Darkness, save for a glowing jack o' lantern. John stands there, listing. Bewildered. Then he switches on a lamp, kicks off his shoes and crashes onto his lumpy old recliner.

JOHN
All right ... You can all come out now ...
Still no reply. John sneers, flicks on the television with the remote control and settles back into his chair.

INSERT - TELEVISION
A scene from another horror movie. A boy shreds his pumpkin mask as a mass of beetles and snakes pour out of his skull.

BACK TO SCENE
JOHN
What is this shit?
Disgusted, he switches channels to the local NEWS. A shrill BEEP from the kitchen startles him. The microwave.

KITCHEN
John waddles to a drawer and removes a set of utensils. Then he reaches for the microwave, opens it. But his dinner is gone.
Spinning around, he sees the piping hot entree already sitting out on the kitchen table. John double takes, mentally retracing his steps. Shrugs.

FOLLOW JOHN as he picks up his tray and plods back down the hall. Suddenly he trips over something the suitcase Debra had packed earlier, sitting smack dead in the center of the hall.

JOHN
So this is the game you wanna play. Fine. Go ahead. Keep it up all night ...

LIVING ROOM
John settles back into his chair and begins to eat ravenously.
SCREAMS from the television. He reacts.

INSERT - TELEVISION
Someone has switched it back to the horror movie. A
COMPUTER GENERATED PUMPKIN causes more masked heads to EXPLODE.

BACK TO SCENE
John shakes the remote. Out of the corner of his eye, he catches a shadowy figure darting by in the darkened foyer.

JOHN

Is that you, you little brat? Danny?!

John rises, about to go for him when suddenly the power cuts out and the entire house is plunged into blackness.

JOHN
(continuing)
When I get my hands on you, kid, you're gonna wish you were never born!

John pulls a rechargeable flashlight from the wall and goes to the cellar door. It stands open. An invitation to enter.

JOHN
(continuing)
Oh, I'm scared. I'm really scared.

With that, John steps down into the basement.

INT. CELLAR (CONTINUOUS)

John tentatively descends the stairs. Barefoot. The flashlight beam preceding his every step. A RUMBLING below.

The cellar is lit only by a shaft of moonlight cutting through the single dusty window. John probes around, shining the flashlight over cobwebs, boxes the puddle of water at his feet. Now flooding the entire floor.

John SLOSHES through the water toward the washing machine which is running at full tact.

JOHN
What the hell

He opens the washer lid and lifts out a water logged sheet. It drips red onto the white appliance blood.

John backs away, loses his footing, and slips in the water landing right at the Shape's feet. John SCREAMS as the Shape grabs him by the neck, lifts him off the floor with one hand, then carries him across the basement and SLAMS him brutally against the open fuse box.

The Shape's free hand lifts an enormous butcher knife. A loud WHAP as it's driven to the hilt into John's chest, through the fuse box.

Sparks wain from the wall. Electricity courses through John's writing body.

EXT. MYERS HOUSE (SAME)

Lights flash on and off in the windows. Suddenly the entire house is plunged into darkness.

INT. MYERS HOUSE - CELLAR (SAME)

John's toes curl. The skin around where the knife penetrates
FRIES. The Shape steps back, head tilted, BREATHING steadily, curiously observing John's hanging, lifeless body.

EXT. HARVEST FAIR - NIGHT

Tommy grabs the ticket he's just paid for, hands it to an ATTENDANT and moves through the turnstiles amid a steady stream of REVELLERS.
Loud MUSIC, the aroma of apple cider and pumpkin pie fills the air.
Booths selling food and crafts. Children carving jack o' lanterns.
Parents beaming with pride.
Trendy co eds playing games. Ducking for apples. Shooting pumpkin faced balloons with water pistols.

EXT. LIBRARY STEPS
Tim and Beth sit on either side of Harry as he interviews them during a live BROADCAST. A large crowd gathered below.

HARRY SIMMS
(into mike)
I'm here with Tim and Beth the organizers of tonight's event. How does it feel knowing you've finally pulled Halloween out of the closet?

TIM
(into mike)
Yo, Harry, it's great! And having you here with us is dope. Totally raw. You're the ultimate juice!

HARRY SIMMS
I'll remember that the next time my wife tells me I didn't make her climax.

BETH
(impassioned)
What Tim means is that we've taken a firm stand against censorship. Not only for Haddonfield, but for every town in the nation. Our generation will not let the powers that be control our minds, dictate what clothes we wear, what music we listen to, or what holidays we celebrate.
Beth's rousing speech is met by gales of enthusiastic CHEERS.

HARRY
(off handedly)
Have you ever considered running for public office?

EXT. HADDONFIELD STREETS - VARIOUS SHOTS - NIGHT
The distant SOUNDS of the celebration are carried on the wings of the WIND. Howling through dark, empty streets. Rows of deserted houses. Not a soul in sight. Preternatural stillness.

INT. BLANKENSHIP HOUSE - NIGHT
Kara looks nervously out a window, then walks into the parlor where she finds Danny sitting in the dark, glued to the Horrorthon.
Flames CRACKLE in the fireplace, casting weird shadows.

Mrs. Blankenship sits in a wooden rocker, cradling the infant, humming a lullaby. If we look closely enough, behind her in the window we can see the hazy shadow of the Shape looking in.

KARA
Mrs. Blankenship, what did you mean about the little boy who used to live across the street?
The old woman doesn't seem to hear her. Lost in her own world.

KARA
(continuing; insistent)
Mrs. Blankenship, please. This is important!
Mrs. Blankenship looks up sharply, startling Kara.

MRS. BLANKENSHIP
He heard the voice. Same as your boy hears.

KARA
What voice? What are you talking about?

MRS. BLANKENSHIP
The voice that spoke to Michael Myers. The one that told him to kill his family.
Kara stares at her, numbed. She gazes over at Danny, his eyes riveted not to the TV screen. Looking past it. Across the street at the Myers house. The haunting VOICE whispers to him.

WHISPERING VOICE (V.O.)
I'm coming for you, Danny ... I'm coming.

EXT. HARVEST FAIR - NIGHT
Tim and Beth ride high atop the Ferris wheel. Their smiling faces aglow in a dizzying whirlwind of LIGHTS. DARK CLOUDS are gathering in the sky, covering the moon and stars. A light RAIN begins to fall.

ANGLE ON TOMMY
Walking, searching, hunting. Past a large tent where children are gathering. A sign reads: COSTUME PAGEANT.
Tommy reacts to a terrified SCREAM. Just a couple of teenage BOYS pulling an innocuously fightened GIRL onto another ride.

THE STRANGER walks steadily past the bright lights of the Ferris wheel.

TOMMY pushes through a dense crowd. Suddenly he bumps shoulders with the Stranger. More people pass. There was something very sinister about that man. Tommy turns to look again, eyes widening in terror.

TOMMY'S P.O.V. - STRANGER'S WRIST
Branded with the mark of Thorn!

TOMMY removes his gun. Flows through the crowd like a vengeful wraith.
People see the gun in his hand and back away. Tommy surges forward. The Stranger walks faster. Gaining ground. Toward the
Halloween tree.
WORKERS hauling wheelbarrows loaded with jack o' lanterns cross his path. Tommy stumbles, pumpkins spilling out all around him.
The Stranger is getting away! Tommy picks himself up, raises the gun and begins FIRING shots into the air. People SCREAM, scattering like insects, ducking for cover.

TOMMY
Stop that man! Stop him!!!
Tommy races through the horrified crowd. The Stranger keeps moving, never once looking back.
Suddenly SIRENS. Squad cars converge. Sheriff Holdt and a slew of
OFFICERS surround Tommy. Weapons trained.

HOLDT
Throw down the gun! Now!!!
Tommy drops the gun. Puts his arms up in surrender. The cops swarm in, taking him.

TOMMY
Stop that man! He's the one!

ANGLE ON FERRIS WHEEL
Beth and Tim exit the ride and follow the crowd toward the flashing
LIGHTS of the police cruisers.

TIM
Who's gettin' busted?
Beth is stunned to see Tommy being searched spread eagle over the sheriff's car.

BETH
Jesus, that's my neighbor. Tommy.

TIM
Isn't he that psycho who's been spying on my sister?

BETH
(worried)
Kara and Danny never showed up tonight. We'd better go home and check on them. There's nothing else for us to do here.

TIM

But they're gonna light the tree in a few minutes

BETH
(suggestively)
We can light our own tree at home.
She brushes against Tim's crotch and saunters away. Tim glances back at Tommy, then follows her like a hungry puppy.

INT. BLANKENSHIP HOUSE - TOMMY'S APARTMENT - NIGHT
Kara rushes Danny and the baby inside. The old spinster close at her heels. Releasing her dark secret.

MRS. BLANKENSHIP
I was baby sitting for him that night. Little
Mikey Myers from across the street. That's when the voice told him what to do. Same as his great grandfather.

KARA
His what?!

MRS. BLANKENSHIP
Eighteen ninety five. A hundred years ago to this night. All Hallows Eve. Murdered his family in that very same house. Then the townspeople burned him alive. Our mother always told us when we were children, 'Don't go near the Myers house.' We never did.

EXT. HARVEST FAIR - NIGHT (SAME)
The Stranger glides unnoticed among a large crowd gathered for the lighting of the Halloween tree. People putting up umbrellas. A
STORM fast approaching.
Hundreds of anxious kids stand beneath the oak tree with open bags and pillow cases, waiting for the candy to drop on them.

STALKING P.O.V
MOVING behind the tree where a long haired figure stands in the darkness. Waiting to make a presentation.

HARRY turns, sensing a presence. A knife shoots out of the darkness, jabbing him right between the legs.

TOMMY is shoved into the back of the squad car. Suddenly Loomis appears. Prevailing upon the sheriff.

LOOMIS
Wait! This boy is being placed in my custody.
Tommy looks out, stunned.

HOLDT
What are you trying to pull now, Loomis?

LOOMIS
Uncuff him! This is a matter of life or death.

SHOCK
HARRY
The knife is lifted straight up, splitting his torso in two, eyes bugging with shock. He slumps to the ground in a huge pool of blood.

CUT BACK TO:
TOMMY AND LOOMIS
The sheriff uncuffs Tommy and shoves him out of the car.

HOLDT
You'd better as fuck have an explanation for this, Doctor.
Loomis begins to usher Tommy through the gaping crowd.

TOMMY
Dr. Loomis, there's something you should know
Tommy is prodded forward by Loomis's .357.

LOOMIS
I know enough already. Just shut your mouth and take me to that baby.
They move swiftly through the gaping crowd.

ANGLE ON TREE
A growing murmur of concern spreads. "Where's Harry?" The children are becoming impatient, and the impending STORM isn't doing much to calm anyone's nerves. Harry's people are at a loss to explain their star's whereabouts.

ANGLE ON LOOMIS AND TOMMY
On the fringes of the crowd. Walking away.
"Oohs" and "ahhs" as the tree suddenly comes to life with thousands of orange lights. From the boughs of the tree, ropes are pulled. Bunting tears open, dropping hails of CANDY on the SHRIEKING kids.
Tommy glances back. His eyes drawn to something. Grotesque and misshapen. In the tree.

TOMMY
Oh my God

ANGLE ON TREE
Kids of all ages scurry around the stage, laughing and screaming as a rainbow of candy RAINS down on them. Diving for it. Fighting over it.

Scooping it up in big handfuls.

ANGLE ON TOMMY AND LOOMIS
Tommy instantly breaks away and tears back through the crowd.

LOOMIS
Tommy!
Loomis goes for him. Sheriff Holdt sees what is happening and flies toward them in pursuit.

ANGLE ON TREE
A BALLERINA looks down at her white pillow case in horrified astonishment. Her hands painted red as she reaches inside. All of her candy is covered with blood!
The other kids back away in revulsion the entire stage begins to drip with blood!
The adults don't seem to notice what is happening, more concerned with the sudden burst of POURING RAIN.
Tommy pushes his way through the crowd, SCREAMING.

TOMMY
Get them out of there! Get out!!!
Sheriff Holdt tries to intercept Tommy just as he leaps up onto the stage, pushing kids out of the way.
Parents' faces register shock when they see their children running toward them, SCREAMING hysterically, soaked with blood.
Loomis sees what Tommy sees. Words cannot convey the horror in his eyes.
Just then, a BOLT OF LIGHTNING ignites the tree. SPARKS flash.
Tiny pumpkin lights EXPLODE in a startling chain reaction.
Tommy helps the last of the kids off the stage when something falls from the gnarled branches: a dangling, rotating, wrapped up thing.
The mutilated remains of Harry Simms!
Horrified, Tommy dashes headlong off the stage. Runs with Loomis with the trampling crowd.
Struck dumb with terror, Holdt looks out upon the mass destruction.
The bloody corpse hanging from the tree. People running, SCREAMING, carrying their children toward the exits.

EXT. CAMPUS PARKING LOT (SAME)
Bumper to bumper cars. Horns BLARING. Women SCREAMING. Men SHOUTING. Children CRYING. Pandemonium.
Loomis and Tommy appear out of this jumble of confusion. More people running along the sidewalks.

TOMMY
Oh, God Kara!!!
A car SCREECHES to a halt as Tommy barrels across the street. Loomis right behind him. Running toward home.

Once again, terror reigns in Haddonfield, Illinois.

INT. BLANKENSHIP HOUSE - TOMMY'S APARTMENT - NIGHT
Kara shivers as she curls up beside Danny on the futon, holding the sleeping baby close at her bosom. THUNDER rattles the old house.

DANNY
Mommy, I'm scared.

KARA
There's nothing to be scared of, baby. It's just another storm. Try to get some sleep.

DANNY
I can't. The voice man is coming to get me.

KARA
No one's coming to get you. Not while I'm around.

DANNY
Promise?

KARA
(kisses him)
I promise.
Kara stands up and goes to the window, looking out into the pouring RAIN.

KARA'S P.O.V. - THE MYERS HOUSE
Dark and foreboding. LIGHTNING FLASHES. Beth's car parked in front.

ANGLE ON KARA
She stares at the car, puzzled. Quickly she moves away from the window, heads out the door.

HALLWAY
She KNOCKS loudly on the door across the hall. A sign that reads: "Beth's Place."

KARA
Beth, are you in there?
She knocks again. No response. Another CLAP OF THUNDER. Kara shudders, quickly returns to Tommy's apartment and locks the door.

INT. MYERS HOUSE - FOYER (CONTINUOUS)
Sounds of PASSION as we FOLLOW a trail of hastily discarded costume pieces across the darkened foyer. Tim and Beth are on the stairs, half naked, kissing fervently.

BETH
(coming up for air)
Guess they went to the fair after all.

TIM
(hot and heavy)
Guess so ...
Tim nuzzles his face in Beth's chest. She's feeling apprehensive.

BETH
What if your parents come home?

TIM
Then they can watch.
Laughing, they heard up the stairs, kissing, fondling each other.
Slowly we PULL BACK into the foyer. THUNDER and LIGHTNING CLASH, revealing the Shape, knife held at ready. Watching.

INT. TOMMY'S APARTMENT (SAME)
She picks up the cordless phone, switches on and dials her home number. We HEAR the phone RINGING on the other end.

INT. MYERS HOUSE - KARA'S BEDROOM - NIGHT
Beth collapses with Tim onto Kara's bed. The PHONE RINGS. Tim ignores it, consumed by passion. Beth sits up nervously.

BETH
Aren't you gonna answer that?

TIM
Answer what?

BETH
(fends him off)
What if it's Kara?
Frustrated, Tim jumps off the bed and stomps into the bathroom, taking a candle with him.

TIM
Fine. You answer it. I'll make friends with my soap on a rope.
Tim slams the door. Beth deliberates her move, then goes to pick up the phone.

BETH
(into phone)
Hello?

INT. TOMMY'S APARTMENT
Kara is frantic. Looking out the window at the Myers house.

KARA
(into phone)
Mom Who is this?

BETH (V.O.)
Kara? ... No, this is Beth.

KARA
What are you doing there? Where's my mother?

INT. MYERS HOUSE - KARA'S BEDROOM (SAME)
BETH
We were worried about you guys so we left early to see if you were

KARA (V.O.)
Is Tim there?

BETH
He's in the bathroom.

BATHROOM - SHOWER (CONTINUOUS)
A lighted candle flickers. Tim waits for the running shower to warm up as he does a bare ass jig over to the sink.
Rinsing off his tooth brush, he elbows out a circle of steam from the mirror. He gasps. The Shape is standing right behind him!
Before he can react, Tim's head is yanked backwards. The chilling
SNAP of his neck is punctuated by a CRASH OF THUNDER.

INT. TOMMY'S APARTMENT
Kara can SEE Beth on the phone. Sitting by the window.

KARA
I'm across the street. I can see you. Beth, I want you to listen to me. Get Tim and get out of that house. Right now.
Unnoticed by Kara, Danny rises and crosses the room. Drawn toward the door by the irascible voice.

WHISPERING VOICE (V.O.)
Come to me, Danny ... Come to me.

INT. MYERS HOUSE - KARA'S BEDROOM
Beth shifts nervously, looking out across the way at Kara.
THUNDER drowns out the sound of the bathroom door CREAKING open. The

Shape advances.

BETH
Kara, what the hell is going on?

INT. TOMMY'S APARTMENT
Kara's mouth suddenly drops open. Her mind snaps into sensory overload.
She can see the Shape walking up behind Beth! Raising a gleaming butcher knife!

KARA
Beth, look out! There's someone in the room! He's right behind you!

INT. MYERS HOUSE - KARA'S BEDROOM
Beth drops the phone, eyes bulging as the Shape plunges the knife into her back. She falls, CRASHING against the vanity.
Beth SCREAMS unholy terror. But the Shape isn't through.

INT. TOMMY'S APARTMENT
Kara stands frozen in pure horror, hearing and seeing her friend's vicious murder.
Her eyes shoot down. A little blond haired boy is walking steadily across the street toward the Myers house.
No, it can't be true. Kara wheels around. Danny is gone.

INT. MYERS HOUSE - KARA'S BEDROOM - ANGLE THROUGH WINDOW
Danny can be seen below walking toward the house as Beth's blood gurgling SCREAMS fill the room. The knife repeatedly, mercilessly SLASHING down at her.

EXT. STREET / MYERS HOUSE - NIGHT
Kara bolts out of the Blankenship house and races across the street, chasing after Danny through RAIN and LIGHTNING.

KARA
Danny, no!!!

KARA'S P.O.V. - FOLLOWING DANNY
He glides up the porch steps and slips through the front door of the
Myers house. Disappearing inside.

KARA shoots across the lawn. Up the porch steps. Right behind him.

INT. MYERS HOUSE - FOYER
Kara dives through the front door. THUNDER shatters the house.
Everything is frighteningly dark. Shockingly quiet.
Inch by inch, she makes her way inside. Eyes wide. Savage.
Shaking uncontrollably. A CRASHING SOUND behind her. She jumps out of her skin.
Just the door SLAMMING shut in the WIND.

KARA
(the faintest whisper)
Danny?
She advances into the hall. Old floorboards CREAK beneath her feet.
SOUNDS up ahead. FOOTSTEPS.
Kara looks up. LIGHTNING FLASHES. Danny is nearing the top of the stairs!
Instinct propels her up the stairs after him. Then suddenly she stops dead. Reason taking over. And she turns back.
Picks up a fireplace poker sitting in the corner. Then she heads back up the stairs. Mind blown with horror.

UPSTAIRS HALLWAY
Kara reaches the top of the staircase, looking down the dark hallway.
Summoning all of her courage, she moves forward.
Suddenly Danny darts out from the adjacent hall and disappears inside his bedroom a fleeting, ghostly image. Kara startles. Follows him inside.

DANNY'S BEDROOM
Danny stands in a corner. LIGHTNING illuminates his toy dinosaurs.
Kara goes to him, takes his hand. He resists her.

KARA
(intense whisper)
Come on ... Danny, please.
She picks him up, carries him toward the door. LUMBERING FOOTSTEPS.
Kara stands paralyzed in the doorway as the Shape stalks down the hall.
Eyes probing. Walking right past them.

DANNY'S BEDROOM
Kara slips silently back into the room, carrying Danny through the bathroom. Adjoining on the opposite side into

KARA'S ROOM
LIGHTNING CRACKLES. The walls are covered with blood. Kara stumbles over something on the floor. Cranes her neck to look down.
Beth's bloody, mangled remains at her feet.
Shock waves send Kara reeling backwards against the open bathroom door.
Hanging on a hook is Tim's naked body, eyes open, staring at her in a horrified rictus of death.
Kara SCREAMS. Drops Danny. Quickly covers her mouth. Realizing that she's given them away.
Suddenly the bedroom door tears open, buckling off its hinges. The
Shape bulldozes in, wielding its huge butcher knife!

KARA

Danny, run!!!
Danny ducks into the hall, evading the Shape's lurching hands.

DANNY careens down the stairs. THUNDER RAGES.

KARA brandishes the fireplace poker at the killer. The Shape moves in, backing her through the bathroom ... into Danny's room. Suddenly she SLAMS the door on the Shape.
Kara tears off into the hallway. Turns. Waiting for the Shape to appear. It doesn't.
Kara vacillates down the hall. Jumping at every sound. Training her weapon at things unseen. SLAMMING doors along the way, sealing off every passageway as she tries to find her way through the impenetrable dark tunnel.
Suddenly something CRASHES down from above. Kara's mother, strung up on a bloody sheet, dangling upside down from the trap door in the ceiling!
The axe still protruding from her chest.

ANOTHER ANGLE
Kara SCREAMS, shrinking away from the gruesome sight, faltering through the blackened doorway behind her. An unbearable moment of tension as we think the Shape's mask will be there.
Suddenly the Shape shoots up directly in front of her! Tearing the dangling corpse from the sheet, dislodging the axe from Debra's chest with a repulsive SQUISH.
Kara wheels toward the stairs. The Shape advances. Swings the axe.
Misses her by inches. Kara ducks, lurches behind the Shape. Swings the fireplace poker with everything she's got. CRACKING it full force over the back of the Shape's head.
The Shape breaks through the banister and plunges off the landing,
SLAMMING hard onto the floor below.
Terrified, Kara chances a look down. The Shape doesn't move.

EXT. STREET / BLANKENSHIP HOUSE - NIGHT (SAME)
Tommy's Explorer skids to a stop outside the boarding house. Loomis and
Tommy fly up the front path. Tommy glances back at the blackened Myers house for a moment, then follows Loomis inside.

INT. MYERS HOUSE - DOWNSTAIRS HALLWAY (SAME)
Kara barrels off the stairs. Moves cautiously past the Shape. Sprawled face up in the middle of the hall.

LIVING ROOM
Kara searches for Danny, keeping her eyes trained on the Shape. The little boy appears in the doorway directly across the hall.
The Shape lying in between them.

KARA
Danny, come to Mommy.
Danny shakes his head. Too frightened to move.

HALLWAY / FOYER

Ever so slowly, Kara moves toward the threshold. Hefting the fireplace poker, she steps right over the Shape.
Instantly she snatches Danny up in her arms. Takes one step forward when suddenly

DANNY

Mommy!!!

The Shape springs up, twisting Kara's ankle. She falls, splaying forward.
The Shape claws at her leg. Kara fights back, kicking herself free of the vice like grip. Scrambling to her feet, Kara rockets Danny through the foyer to the front door desperately trying to escape from this real life house of horrors
only to find that it is locked.
The Shape rises, gleaming butcher knife in hand.
Kara twists the deadbolt, but someone's secured the chain lock! Too late to remove it. The Shape is right behind them.
Only one way to go. The cellar. Kara shoves Danny through.

INT. CELLAR (CONTINUOUS)

Kara and Danny clatter down the rickety stairs and SPLASH across the flooded basement floor.
A soul shuddering POUNDING on the door above.
Kara ushers Danny toward the elevated window.
The cellar door EXPLODES, the Shape's hand breaking through, splintering the wood as if it were paper.
Kara HEARS the Shape moving rapidly down the stairs. Lifts Danny up the wall toward the window. But it's not a wall it's John's electrocuted body, propped inside a storage cabinet!
Danny SHRIEKS, staring into John's lifeless eyes. Kara pushes him up.
Danny reaches for the lock. Just an inch away.
Kara can't lift him any higher. The Shape is coming!
Danny hoists himself up just enough to twist the lock. He pushes the window open and clambers outside.
Kara scrambles up old pressboard shelves. They break under her weight; she topples back to the floor.
The Shape wades toward her. Reaching up for the window.

EXT. MYERS HOUSE - BASEMENT WINDOW

Danny watches his mother struggle to climb out of the crypt.

KARA

Danny, help me!

Kara's hand reaches toward him. Danny makes no movement.

WHISPERING VOICE (V.O.)

Come to me, Danny ... Come to me.

Danny obediently turns and starts to walk away.

KARA
Danny!!!

INT. MYERS HOUSE - CELLAR
Kara's foot falls on the handle of the knife jutting from her father's chest. Uses it to springboard herself half way through the window.
Clawing at wet grass.
The Shape's hand shoots out of the darkness below, grabbing at her legs.
Kara writhes, kicking and SCREAMING.

EXT. MYERS HOUSE - CELLAR WINDOW
Kara grabs chunks of mud as she is pulled back through the window. The
Shape yanks hard. Kara catches herself on the window frame. Quickly losing her grip.

INT. MYERS HOUSE - CELLAR
The knife swipes downward, swiping her ankle.

EXT. MYERS HOUSE - CELLAR WINDOW
Kara reacts to the searing pain, releasing her grip on the window frame.
Suddenly Danny appears, locking onto her collar, pulling her clear in one massive heave.
Kara shuffles across the ground and picks herself up. Grabs Danny's hand and runs full tilt around the side of the house.

EXT. STREET / BLANKENSHIP HOUSE
CAMERA FOLLOWS their frenzied flight across the street. Past Tommy's
Explorer. Kara limping. Danny surging toward the Blankenship house. Kara
SCREAMS, pounding frantically on the door.

KARA
Please! Open the door!

INT. BLANKENSHIP HOUSE - TOMMY'S APARTMENT
Tommy and Loomis have turned the apartment upside down.

TOMMY
The baby where's the baby?!
Suddenly they HEAR Kara's frantic pleas outside. Tommy bolts out the door.
Loomis right behind him.

EXT. BLANKENSHIP HOUSE (CONTINUOUS)
Kara POUNDS furiously.

KARA

Please! Somebody help us!
Danny huddles beside her, peering out across the street.

DANNY'S P.O.V. - MYERS HOUSE
The Shape trudges boldly down the porch steps knife in hand!

BACK TO SCENE
Kara sees the Shape walking slowly and deliberately toward them. Her SCREAMS become even more intense.

KARA
Help us please!!!
The Shape closes in. At the last second, Tommy throws open the door. Kara and Danny tumble inside. Into his arms.

INT. BLANKENSHIP HOUSE - LOBBY / PARLOR (CONTINUOUS)
Loomis slams and deadbolts the door.

LOOMIS
Get them upstairs. Now!
Kara pounds against Tommy's chest. Hysterical.

KARA
Where's the baby?!

TOMMY
He's gone.
Kara holds Danny close to her side, backing away in horror as Tommy and Loomis go around the parlor, securing the doors and windows. THUNDER RIPS through the darkened room.

TOMMY
(continuing)
Who else knew I had the baby?!

LOOMIS
No one.

TOMMY
No there had to be someone else. Who knew?!

LOOMIS
Only me
(dark realization)
and Dr. Wynn.

Suddenly the window behind Kara EXPLODES. She SCREAMS, recoiling. Then the window in front of her. HANDS reach through. Tommy shoves her out of the way. ANOTHER HAND shoots through the stained glass window in the front door, twists open the lock.

Danny races across the lobby and up the stairs.

Robed figures fill the doorways. Climbing through windows. Moving inside the house. Surrounding Loomis.

LOOMIS
(continuing)
Wynn!!!

The robed figures descend on Loomis. Drops his .357. Tommy lurches for it, to no avail. Loomis's SCREAM fills the darkness like a fever dream.

LOOMIS
(continuing)
Run, Tommy!!! Run!!!

TOMMY
No!!!

Tommy backpedals up the stairs. Kara pulling him along as the cloaked figures glow toward them. Daggers raised.

UPSTAIRS HALLWAY
Kara reacts to the SOUND of Danny's VOICE.

DANNY
Mommy! Please help me!

Kara rushes through darkness to find him.

KARA
Danny! Danny, where are you?!

TOMMY
Kara, no!

Kara trips and falls. A pair of silver tipped black boots planted in bold stance. Slowly she looks up the long duster, the cigarette in the gloved hand of the nefarious Stranger Dr. Wynn! Danny stands by his side, staring dispassionately.

KARA
Danny, no ... please ...

Kara picks herself up, shaking her head in unmitigated fear, staggering back down the hallway.

She turns to see the black figures overtaking Tommy. His SCREAMS swallowed by hollow darkness.

Alone, Kara careens through another doorway into

TOMMY'S APARTMENT
Kara slams the door, turns in desperate circles.
Stepping out from behind the door is Mrs. Blankenship the baby bundled in her arms!

KARA
Mrs. Blankenship Oh, God Hurry. We have to
As Kara reaches for the baby, the old woman raises a dagger. Her eyes burning. Her wrist branded with the mark of Thorn!
Kara SCREAMS. The old woman opens the door, allowing the figures to enter the room. Daggers drawn. CHANTING a dark invocation.
The coven forces Kara backwards. Nowhere to run. Nowhere to hide.
Suddenly Kara makes a decision and takes a running leap toward the window!

EXT. BLANKENSHIP HOUSE (CONTINUOUS)
Defenestrating herself, Kara SCREAMS, tumbling through the air, bouncing off the porch overhang before plunging to the front lawn below. A thousand grass fragments raining down on her.

KARA lies on her back, eyes close, hands folded over her chest in silent repose. She doesn't move.

THE HOUSE is still. Unearthly silence fills the cold October night.

SLOW DISSOLVE TO:
KARA'S P.O.V. - DISTORTED - INT. TUNNELS
A ring of faceless figures move in, completely surrounding her.
Suddenly the feeling of RAPID MOVEMENT. Glowing torchlight flickers across dank walls.

KARA is being pushed forward on a gurney. Strapped down. SCREAMING for God's mercy.

TOMMY is wheeled through another tunnel. His face a mass of bloody cuts and bruises. His eyes glazed over, trying to find focus. SLAMMING into darkness.

EXT. SANITARIUM - NIGHT
LIGHTNING illuminates the cold, forbidding asylum. The white van pulls up to the security gate. Headlights illuminate the sign: "SMITH'S GROVE

WARREN COUNTY SANITARIUM."
The main gate cranks open. The van pulls through.

THE VAN pulls to a stop near the main building. The door slides open and Danny steps out, surrounded by Smith's Grove staff wearing white jackets.
Leading him toward the entrance.

LANDING FIELD
The helicopter touches down. Wynn ducks out, moving in long, even strides toward the building.

INT. SANITARIUM CORRIDOR - NIGHT
FOLLOW Wynn through the series of security cages, using his key card to
BUZZ through. White coats bringing up the rear.
Through tall mahogany doors, they cross purposefully into the adjacent wing.

EXECUTIVE RECEPTION AREA
Dawn, Wynn's efficient secretary, rises with a congenial smile.

DAWN
Good evening, Dr. Wynn. Your appointment is waiting inside.
Wynn picks up his messages, then heads straight into the office. Dawn resumes her typing. Something eerie in her grin.

INT. WYNN'S OFFICE - NIGHT (CONTINUOUS)
Wynn and his staff file inside. Removing his hat and duster, he walks over to where Loomis is seated shackled to a chair, a bloody slash across his forehead.
Seeing this, Wynn snaps angrily at two burly GUARDS.

WYNN
What is this all about? Remove those!
The guards comply. Loomis rubs his aching wrists, glowering.

LOOMIS
Where's the child?

WYNN
Sam, you know you never fail to amaze me. Yesterday happily retired, today right back in the thick of things.
Somehow I knew you still had it in you.
Loomis sees his .357 resting atop Wynn's desk only inches away. Wynn's hand covers it, slips it inside the top drawer.

WYNN
(continuing)
Come now, Sam. This is a gathering of old friends. I know how difficult this must be for you a man of your upbringing and integrity but now that I'm in charge I felt it was only fair that you finally know the truth.
(gestures to his staff)
After all, you're the only one around here who's still in the dark, as it were. This isn't the way I wanted to tell you, but you've really given me no other choice.

LOOMIS
This is madness, Wynn.

WYNN
Your madness is another man's greatness. This is the way things have always been. You've just been too blinded by your own reality to see.
(beat)
But having you on the outside has been convenient for us in many ways.
(smiles)
You always did come through our loyal watch dog.
Finding him. Bringing him back to us once he'd finished his work. Although after you had that nasty stroke the last time, I had to go after him myself. And what a terrible time we had getting him out of that jail cell.

LOOMIS
It was you.

WYNN
(lights a cigarette)
Sometimes a cigar is just a cigar.

LOOMIS
Why did you take Jamie?

WYNN
She has the gift the blood of Thorn running through her veins. Michael's mother had it, too. So for six years I incubated her, prepared her for this night. Michael has served his purpose. And soon we will have a new progeny.

LOOMIS
Jamie's baby ...

WYNN
There you go trying to make sense again.
(grimly entranced)
It's a curse. Handed down through countless generations.
As ageless as this celebration which you call Halloween.

LOOMIS
Samhain.

WYNN
And I'm its deliverer.
(slams his key card on the desk)
Its calling card, if you will. I follow it. Protect it.
Act as its guardian. In a sense, Sam, so do you.

Loomis shudders, rocked by these revelations.

WYNN
(continuing)
I know you have more questions, my friend, and there's so much more for you to try to make sense of.

Loomis is hoisted out of his chair and led out of the office. Wynn and his white coats flow out behind him.

INT. CELL - NIGHT

A tight, damp, claustrophobic space. Tommy is strapped upright to a crude metal rack, not unlike the one Jamie was bound to the night before.

Feverishly he rubs his wrists against a jagged metal edge, cutting through skin, wearing away his bonds. Breaking through.

INT. TUNNELS - NIGHT (CONTINUOUS)

A group of white coats, led by Wynn, usher Loomis off an old service elevator, leading him through the dark passageway. Wynn turns around, surveying the tunnel. As he walks on, we SEE something fall from his back pocket.

As they disappear down another tunnel, a wooden door slowly CREAKS open.

Tommy appears, cautiously stepping out into the catacombs. Edging along the dank, torch lit walls. WIND MOANS. Rats scamper past his feet.

Wynn has dropped his security key card. Tommy swipes it.

INT. CATWALK (SAME)

Loomis is led across a narrow precipice overlooking a filthy prison cell.

The Shape lies inside. Dormant.

Wynn stares down hypnotically at his most prized possession. Michael Myers.

WYNN
Look at him. So silent, yet so deadly. He moves when I tell him to. Act on my impulses. Feels what I feel.

Wynn demonstrates. Loomis looks on, spellbound.

WYNN
(continuing)
Michael Rise.

Below, the Shape slowly rises. Wynn takes out his trusted switchblade.

WYNN
(continuing)
Michael Pain.

Wynn cuts his hand. The Shape grabs his own hand in agony. Wynn smiles, sucking the bleeding gash.

WYNN

(continuing)
Michael Kill.
Suddenly Wynn whirls around, throwing Dawn his faithful secretary inside the Shape's pit. Wynn watches with hideous delight as her horrified
SCREAMS trail away into blood gurgling SILENCE.
Loomis closes his eyes in anguish.

LOOMIS
You've created a monster.

WYNN
Amazing, isn't it? I even taught him to drive.
Wynn carries on without remorse. Loomis is brutally shoved forward.

WYNN
(continuing)
We're not the only ones, you know. There are many believers generous contributors to our church. You'd be amazed to know how far it reaches.

INT. CATACOMBS - STORAGE BUNKER
A metal door BUZZES open. Tommy makes his way furtively inside, pocketing the key card.
A storage room filled with sawdust and wooden crates. Tommy pries one of them open. Eyes widening in startled disbelief.
A small arsenal of automatic rifles and ammunition inside.

TOMMY
Holy shit ...
Tommy lifts a rifle, awed by its devastating lines, then slams in a cartridge and bolts out the door. Back into the tunnels.

INT. CEREMONIAL ROOM - NIGHT
A large, amber hued chamber. The CHANTING coven forms a circle around a primitive stone altar where Kara is tied down, wearing a white gown, her head adorned with a wreath of mistletoe.
A wooden symbol of Thorn, like an inverted crucifix, hangs in a place of reverence.
Behind the altar, the Shape stands in its cell. Waiting.
Loomis is led inside. Wynn glides through this macabre gathering, up to the altar. Looming over the terrified Kara.
The CHANTING continues as Wynn dons a magnificent ceremonial robe. At
Wynn's gesture, there is SILENCE. The worshippers offer an obedient response, removing their hoods, baring the mark of Thorn on their wrists.
We recognize many of the faces in the congregation. Wynn's staff. Dr.
Bonham. Mrs. Blankenship. The cross eyed attendant from the bus depot.
People from all walks of life.
Faces glazed with sadistic rapture.

WYNN
(prophetically)
Behind, Disciples of Thorn! The final sign! The birth of the heretic child, delivered unto us on the eve of our great Feast of the Sun ... as I have foreseen it.
Jamie's baby is carried forth, CRYING as it is lain inside a baptismal urn beside Kara. Ringed by candles and a circle of stones eleven in all etched with symbolic runes.

INT. TUNNELS
Letting the rifle guide him, Tommy makes his way through the tunnels.
Toward the sound of MUFFLED CHANTING up ahead.

CEREMONIAL ROOM
The coven CHANTS its invocation. Wynn draws a magic circle around the infant with blood from a silver chalice. Then he inscribes a pentagram in the air with an ornate dagger.

WYNN
Spirits and powers of the flame, attend and witness this ritual. Bear our gifts to Thorn. Open us to the path of
Darkness. By these runes transform us. Open our eyes and show us the Chosen One to whom we offer this sacrifice of
Innocent Blood.
Suddenly Danny is issued forth up to the altar. His eyes dark, lifeless pools. Kara struggles against her bonds.

KARA
Danny!!!
Loomis lurches forward. Halted by massive, restraining hands.

CATWALK
Tommy moves cautiously along the narrow wooden lip, looking down upon the evil ritual. Startled by the SOUND of rusted chains. Pulleys CRANKING.
The Shape's cell being opened.

CEREMONIAL ROOM
The Shape emerges from its cell and slowly walks forward. Strangely calm.
Hypnotized. Looming above Kara. She lets out a SCREAM of unbridled terror as he raises a gleaming dagger.
Wynn stands behind Danny. Places the dagger in his hand and holds it aloft.
Above the baby.

WYNN
Strong and fierce Thorn, Thundered, by thy hammer we summon thee and offer this sacrifice of innocent blood. Let thy
Darkness descend on your son. Danny. Lord of the Dead.

Danny drifts into the dark spell, holding the dagger above the SCREAMING infant. Wynn speaks in the ominous WHISPERING VOICE:

WYNN
(continuing)
Kill for him, Danny ... Kill for him.
Kara cries, appealing to the boy inside of Michael.

KARA
Michael, please. You can make him stop. You remember, don't you?
The Shape stares hard at her through the sockets of its mask. Listening.
Reminded of his mother.

KARA
(continuing)
Remember what he did to you that night. What his voice told you to do. You can stop it, Michael. Stop the voice forever.
Danny's eyes flash like fire. The CHANTING is insidious.

WYNN
Kill him, Danny. Kill him!

KARA
Danny, don't listen! The voice isn't real!
Danny turns sharply, seeing his mother. Suddenly terrified.

WYNN
Kill him, Danny! You feel the rage inside! You are Thorn!
Suddenly Danny drops the dagger. Wynn flies at him, SCREAMING like an enraged beast. The Shape raises its dagger and plunges it into Wynn!
Wynn's eyes go wide with shock. The Shape lurches empathetically. Wynn staggers, yanks the blade from his stomach.
RAPID FIRE GUNSHOTS rip through the chamber as Tommy lets loose a barrage of bullets from above. Taking out several coven members, the rest scattering, retreating into the tunnels.
Loomis dives Danny a split second before he through Kara's bonds with the dagger.
Kara springs toward the baby as the room is ripped apart by GUNFIRE. The altar decimated. Candles falling. Setting the room ablaze.
Wynn releases the supports which suspend the catwalk. Wooden girders CRASH down from the ceiling. Tommy pitches to the floor, dropping the rifle.
The Shape staggers, trying to get to its feet. Slowly. Painfully. Flames lapping at its back.
Loomis crawls toward the rifle. Grabs it. Rises just as Wynn seizes Danny, a dagger at his throat. Pulling him away.

LOOMIS

No!!!

WYNN
Stay away, Sam.

LOOMIS
Leave the boy. Take me.
Loomis slowly places the rifle down in front of Wynn. Surrendering himself.
Tommy drags himself toward Kara and the baby. Paralyzed with horror as they try to anticipate Wynn's move.

WYNN
(smiles trenchantly)
Good bye, Dr. Loomis.
Loomis turns. Gasps in startled reflex. The Shape rises up behind him, swiping the dagger across his chest!
Wynn retreats and flies through a doorway with Danny.

DANNY
Mommy!!!

KARA
Danny!!!
Tommy and Kara race across the flame engulfed room, reaching the door just as it SLAMS shut. Cutting them off.
The Shape, the trail of flames growing on its back, hurls Loomis over the crushed altar.
Tommy sees Loomis writhing on the floor, about to go for him when
The Shape turns on them! Tommy stands in front of Kara and the baby, backing away, propelling them out into the tunnels.
The Shape walks forward in fevered pursuit, all but consumed by fire.

TUNNELS
Tommy, Kara and Danny race deep into the heart of the tunnel maze.

LOOMIS painfully crawls away.

LOOMIS
Die, Michael. In the name of God, die!

END OF TUNNEL
Tommy, Kara and Danny reach the tunnel end. Kara pounds frantically on the elevator panel. A DEAFENING ROAR the SOUND of fire as the Shape sweeps toward them.

THE SHAPE glides steadily through the tunnels. A walking pillar of flame. Undaunted. Unstoppable. Hell spawned.

END OF TUNNEL
Finally the doors open. Kara and Tommy barrel inside. Mashing buttons until the doors close a millisecond before the Shape reaches them.

INT. ELEVATOR
Kara cradles the baby. Tommy waits anxiously as the old elevator MOANS and GRINDS toward ground level. The doors open.

INT. SANITARIUM CORRIDOR
They barrel off the elevator and race down a long corridor.

TOMMY
This way!
Tommy leads her toward an exit sign. Behind them, the elevator doors close.
The indicator light shows it moving down.
They reach a dead end. The row of coded security cages.

KARA
What now?!

TOMMY
(realization)
Wait a minute ...
He reaches into his pocket withdrawing Wynn's key card!
Suddenly the elevator doors open. FIRE GUSTS. The Shape emerges, totally engulfed in flame. The emergency sprinklers are activated. Dousing the flames as it walks after them.
Tommy panics, runs the key card. The gate BUZZES open. They run through.
The Shape's hands lurch through the bars, missing Kara by inches.
They race toward the next gate. The gate behind them opens, and the Shape walks through!
Tommy runs the card again. The gate BUZZES. They slam it one step ahead of the Shape.
The third and final gate. Tommy tries the card. Nothing!

KARA
Come on!

TOMMY
(tries it again)
It's not working!
The Shape moves through the last gate. Inside the cage with them!

TOMMY
(continuing)
Someone's controlling it!

INT. WYNN'S OFFICE (SAME)

Standing behind his computer, observing them on the security monitors, Dr. Wynn jams the card's access code. Then he grabs his satchel and strides quickly out of the office. Pulling Danny with him.

On the screens, we can SEE the Shape approaching. Kara's SCREAM can almost be heard on the silent monitor.

INT. SECURITY CAGE (SAME)

Kara SCREAMS as the Shape rakes Tommy against the cage. Kara cowers in the corner, protecting the baby.

EXT. SANITARIUM - FIELD - NIGHT (SAME)

Wynn races with Danny across the field toward the waiting helicopter.

Getting ready for take off as they duck inside.

INT. SECURITY CAGE

The Shape slams Tommy's head against the bars; he slumps to the floor. Then turns its murderous attention on Kara and the baby.

INT. WYNN'S OFFICE

A hand reaches into the top desk drawer, removes the .357 and FIRES an entire round into the security console. Destroying it.

The man holding the gun is Loomis.

INT. SECURITY CAGE

The door BUZZES open. Kara drags Tommy and the baby out. Slamming the door shut on the Shape. Trapping it inside.

The Shape lurches against the bars in wild paroxysms.

EXT. SANITARIUM - LANDING FIELD

Tommy comes to as he races with Kara and the baby across the windswept field.

Suddenly they stop dead, watching in horror as the helicopter lifts off.

Kara stands paralyzed with shock, looking skyward. The helicopter disappears into the gloom filled night.

Tommy drags Kara in another direction. A vehicle parked nearby. The white van.

INT. VAN (SAME)

Kara lifts the baby inside. Tommy flops down in the driver's seat. Face bruised and bloody. A key in the ignition.

Kara holds Jamie's baby. Tears falling.

KARA

How will we ever find him?

Tommy's gaze terrifies her. He starts the engine and tears off toward the sanitarium gate.

Kara looks down at the baby, then stares numbly forward.

In the back of the van, we can SEE the the Shape's white mask. Glowing in the darkness. Emerging.

Kara and Tommy drive on, unaware. And that, for now, is how we leave them.

FADE OUT.

Made in the USA
Monee, IL
14 October 2021